90 Days on the

> Building Health, Wealth, and Abundance
>
> by
>
> Lora Newman, M.S.

Path to Success

Copyrighted Material

90 Days On The Path To Success – Building Health, Wealth, and Abundance
Copyright © 2008 by Lora Newman

ALL RIGHTS RESERVED

No part of this publication may be reproduced, stored in a retrieval system or transmitted, in any form or by any means — electronic, mechanical, photocopying, recording or otherwise — without prior written permission, except for the inclusion of brief quotations in a review.

For information about this title or to order other books and/or electronic media, contact the publisher:
Life University Coaching & Counseling, LLC
www.lifeuniversitycoach.com
www.loranewman.com
(417) 844-6283

ISBN: 978-1-60643-907-4

Printed in the United States of America

Book and Cover design by: Dave Lappin

Acknowledgments and Thanks

God, for guiding me in this writing and journey
called life, even when I wasn't listening.

My husband, son, and mother, for the love and encouragement.

Melody Wood, for giving me the awakening and
courage to take the journey to the next level.

Lyn Allen, for teaching me ease, grace, and joy, as well
as compassion and awareness on the journey.

Dr. Leon Bradshaw and Jane Dosch, for teaching
me to bravely say it as I see it.

Pastor James Buckman, for the spiritual support and many Bible verses.

Neil and Kim McHugh, for offering the best medicine of
laughter and being catalysts in getting this book finished.

Merry Norman, friend and powerful prayer warrior.

My clients, for joining me on the journey.

Before We Begin

Congratulations on taking the first step toward getting more out of your life and more on the bottom line. So many people say they want more out of life, and yet never take any steps in the direction they wish to go.

My hope is that this book/journal will give you information to begin a journey of awakening to truth as well as support you in making changes to move you along your path to success. The first two sections, *To Believe or Not to Believe* and *Accelerate on the Path to Success,* offer information and tools to challenge your beliefs, mostly about yourself. The third section, the 90-day journal, is for you to work toward any goal that you choose. The last two sections, *Resources and Appendix,* provide tools to help you on your journey.

> "There is a difference between
> knowing the path and walking the path."
> —Morpheus, in *The Matrix*

Contents

Introduction 9
The Big Letdown 9
What Is Your Bottom Line? 10
Awakening, Awareness, and Attraction 11

Part 1: To Believe or Not to Believe 13
1. The Power of Belief 15
2. Who Do You Define Yourself As? 19
3. Education and Critical Thinking 21
4. Be a Student 23
5. Attraction, or Living in God Space 25
6. Like Attracts Like: God Space Up Close 29
7. Attitudes of Inertia 33
8. Your Health: Don't Be a Lemming 35
9. Your Wealth: Manifested Energy 41
10. Responsibility, or the Lack Thereof 45
11. Blame, Judgment, and Other Dances in Victimhood ... 47
12. Filling in the Gaps in Life 49
13. Emotional Bondage Vs. Emotional Integrity 53
14. Perpetual Motion: Stop the Clock! 57
15. The Delusion of Control 61
16. Energy Loss: Drains and Distractions 63
17. The Undertow of Thought and Emotion 67
18. The Three Rs 69
19. The Box of Negative Mental Undertow 71
20. The Formula to Neutralize Procrastination 75
21. The Depth of Love and Deserve Level 79

22. Loop of Gratitude and Faith 83
23. Focus: An Investment of Energy 87

Part 2: Accelerate on the Path to Success 91
24. Begin Each Day with Nourishment 93
25. Supercharge Your Energy Investment 95
26. Be the Blessing That You Seek 99
27. Receive 101
28. Be Willing 103
29. Throw Out Your Goals and Set a Destination 105
30. Make It Real: Visualize! 107
31. Consistency and Commitment 109

Part 3: 90-Day Success Work Journal 113

Part 4: Resources 217

Part 5: Appendix 223

Introduction

The Big Letdown

So you've attended the seminar and bought the latest self-help book or CD. You've completed the material—*let the changes begin!* Wait a minute. It has been a month since the "go-getter seminar," and nothing is changing like you thought it would. You may think, "What is going on? That was a rip-off! I did all of the exercises and nothing happened!" *What compels you to look outside yourself for the answers? Change begins within.*

Life is a process, ever changing. There is no magical formula or pill that will forever change you, with the exception of God's intervention. I wish a magic wand existed, but Disney holds the patent on that. You have to be willing to change on a moment-to-moment basis. This means that your everyday thinking has to shift.

You choose how you react or respond to each and every moment. When you make changes and meet resistance, the tendency is to fall back to that familiar safety and revert to the old ways of being and thinking. What has changed? The old pattern is showing up right on schedule.

You will meet resistance. Things and people may not do what you want them to. Let go. When you move into the perception of control, you set yourself up for frustration and disappointment.

When you choose to release or shed old paradigms, habits, and behaviors, the things and people around you will change. Expect it. It looks scary at first, because the people and dynamics may go away. What does this mean? Are you being abandoned? No! You are releasing what you no longer want or what no longer supports your growth, and this creates space for whom and what you do want.

This transformation may not occur when and how you want it to, but know that all things happen when you create space in your life for it to happen. God's reality is wonderful! Create the space for miracles and walk in faith; God will fulfill your desires. Let go. You will land in a better place than you ever imagined. He never ceases to amaze me, because he knows me better than I do.

Bible Passage: Luke 12:32

What is Your Bottom Line?

What I hear most often from people is, "I want more…" The common endings to that statement are happiness, money, freedom, energy, health, abundance, time, space, confidence, consistency, and love, just to name a few.

Sometimes we can become quite "fix-it" oriented. We fix symptoms with pills, techniques, or money. Symptoms manifest in physical and mental health, marriage, finances, legal situations, and moral or spiritual issues. The unfortunate thing is that we tend to mask the real issues by soothing the symptoms. We think that we can change or tweak one aspect and our life will be "fixed." One example is weight loss. Some people believe that losing 40 pounds or even 10 pounds will make them happy and change their life. The underlying factors to being overweight and unhappy are ignored, and the change is not sustainable. Happiness goes out the window as disappointment sets in. Or another scenario might involve the individual who declares, "If my spouse would change, then I could find happiness." Huh? Hello, Houston, we have a problem.

So often, the root of the problem is multifaceted, meaning that we need to make changes in more than one area of life. I will be addressing many facets as we go along in this book. We are complicated beings. We have mind, body, and spirit to tend to. When one area gets out of balance, the others usually follow. God created a wonderful and beautiful creature in mankind. Some say that space is the final frontier. I don't believe that; the dynamics of mind, body, and spirit are the final frontier. We know very little about the dynamics of the human mind. The one thing we know is that you have a choice in every waking moment. You can choose to make the changes to increase or decrease your bottom line! It is a choice. What do you choose right now?

Awakening, Awareness, and Attraction

The very act of purchasing this book shows that you desire change in some aspect of your life. As we grow and develop—and we all do this throughout our lives—our desires change. What is important tends to change. What meant a lot in your twenties may mean nothing to you in your forties.

At some point in life, you may begin to re-evaluate the course you are on. You may wake up one day and look around to see that you desire something more or different in life. The awakening has occurred, and the journey can then begin.

Awakenings happen at different points in life for different people. Some experience an awakening after a life-threatening event, such as a health crisis. Others have a life-altering event like divorce or the loss of a loved one. Some just wake up one day and decide that they desire more in their lives. Whatever the impetus, a step is taken through a new door.

My journey began in a weekend workshop. I had my first awakening to thinking and being in a different way. I learned that my mind thought many things, and I believed everything I thought, which was not moving me in the direction that I wished to go. I learned a process of awareness to support the changes. I have learned to discern my thoughts and feelings and determine whether they are true. Think about the last time you held yourself back from taking a step in the direction you really wanted to go. Many times, we believe the racket in our head and stop short of where we would really like to be.

I was also jolted with a life-altering event that shook my foundation. My father died of lung cancer at the young age of 55. He had his retirement in front of him, and—poof—he was gone. Afterward, I spent time wondering what my purpose was. I felt like I was just floating through life. I had never lost anyone close to me. I began asking God for direction, and began listening for the signs. They came—sometimes as a whisper and sometimes in the form of a holy two-by-four across the forehead.

It doesn't matter what prompted you to want some change in your life. The bottom line is, you wish to grow in a new direction! *Congratulations!* In this book, the process of change is examined, as well as the mental stops that can occur. Many tools are also provided in the *Resources* and *Appendix* sections to support you when you encounter a roadblock on your path to success. You may find yourself resisting change or embracing it with each breath. I wish it were as easy as mindlessly reading some affirmations each morning, but we have to make internal adjustments in thinking and feeling in order to bring about the outward changes that we desire. I am not discounting the value of affirmations, but it takes more than adding a daily ritual to make life-altering, sustainable changes.

Your attitudes toward finances, health, and quality of life are the products of how you think. If you don't like what you see, the change is an inside job! I am not suggesting that you cause ill health or bankruptcy simply with thoughts. It is the thinking that drives the behavior—how you treat your body and money—that leads to problems. Be willing to explore your attitudes and make adjustments along your path to success.

Part 1

To Believe or Not to Believe

Chapter 1

THE POWER OF BELIEF

The journey begins by taking a look at some common beliefs and dynamics in health, wealth, and abundance. There may be areas in your own beliefs and dynamics that need to be challenged in order to bring about change. If you feel frustration or resistance, notice the frustration and resistance and take note of what your mind tries to tell you about the subject matter. Resistance can show up in different ways. For some, it may show up with thoughts that this book is presenting some "crazy" material. For others, frustration or anger may set in as resistance to what is being presented. Simply note any thoughts or feelings that attempt to disregard or negate new ideas. Resistance is usually strongest when the new ways of thinking are actually applied in life.

If resistance shows up, keep reading and imagine how your life might change by believing differently and "being" differently. You don't have to adopt any new ideas or beliefs, just consider a new way of being and living. Where you are in life is the result of the beliefs and decisions you have made on a moment-to-moment basis up to this point. If you don't like where you are in life or an aspect of your life, it is time to examine the beliefs and decisions that are holding you there. Simply begin making different decisions when the opportunity arises. This brings about change one way or another.

The Power of Belief

In order to bring about change, you first must become aware of what is holding you back and needs to be changed. One place to begin is in your belief systems. How you think about and view the world is what manifests your reality. We all have information filters through which incoming information is processed. Some common filters are stereotypes. Finish these statements and examine how you create your reality through the filters you have in place.

Wealthy people _____.

Blondes _____.

Homeless people _____.

Successful people_____.

In order to be successful, I must _____.

Beliefs are powerful. People die for them. People also live miserably in them. You choose what to believe about yourself and your life. If you believe that you will never have the life of your choosing, you probably never will.

A belief system is constructed when we collect a little data and generalize it to fit a category of events, things, or people. A belief can be built with advertising. Look at the beliefs around beauty that are gained from billboards, television, and magazines. Or better yet, check out the political campaigns during the peak of the political season. Talk about a conflict of beliefs.

Personal beliefs (beliefs about yourself) can sometimes be the hardest to break apart. I see people hold onto false beliefs about themselves and struggle to let go of them so that they can build a new definition of themselves. The false personal beliefs hold us back from our greatness and often are held onto because they are familiar; we don't know what it will mean if we let go of them. Have you ever wanted to try something like a different career or going back to school. Did you worry what the people around you would say about it, or worry if you could maintain it, or worry if you could even do it? After all the worry, you didn't do it. You were not believing in yourself. A lack of confidence is nothing more than not trusting yourself to handle whatever comes your way. In an indirect way, it is a lack of trust in God. He provides us with what we need when we need it. That last part, the timing, is the part we struggle with. We think we need it yesterday, and He knows better. I have always found His timing to be perfect, in spite of the fit I threw about it the day before. If you are feeling called to express and use a gift that you have, I challenge you to begin taking the steps toward doing just that. If greatness were always easy, you wouldn't be reading this.

We can deconstruct personal beliefs, but this takes a little effort. When you begin to deconstruct your belief systems, it may feel as if your world has been turned upside down, or it may be joyful. Either way, allow yourself the space to process and grow. After all, you are only human and must deal with your human condition.

The people around you may be uncomfortable with the new and developing you; that is okay. It is also an opportunity for them to redefine themselves and develop new standards. Some may become too uncomfortable and fade into the background of your life. That is okay, too. You have enough of your own negative mental undertow and do not need to add that of a friend.

In the attraction principle, belief is an important ingredient. As I stated before, what you believe will manifest. When working on making changes in anything, we are also results-oriented creatures. We want some proof that whatever we are working toward is happening. This is where we can strengthen the belief muscle. Focus on what you want and *know* that it is on its way. It is here, but you just can't see it yet. That is all. I have a client who is working on manifesting a personal jet. I know it is at the hangar; we simply can't physically see it yet. This client is working on making room in life for the jet to enter.

Release your fear; it is probably nothing more than a false personal belief anyway. Who do you want to give your power to—greatness and glory or fear and scarcity? You choose. What is it that you want and just can't see with your eyes yet? What do you need to shift or let go of to make room for it? Often, it is the false personal beliefs that need to shift or be released, because they are what hold your dreams and destinations at bay.

Bible Passage: Matthew 25:14–30

Chapter 2

WHO DO YOU DEFINE YOURSELF AS?

I wish there was a magic pill that could make us into who we wish to be. That key to this is found within. You see, we all derive a definition of ourselves from moment to moment. It can be situational, such as:

- you are mom or dad to your kids
- wife or husband to your spouse
- son or daughter to your parents
- aunt or uncle
- the hotshot in town
- etc.

On another level, we define ourselves even further, and this is the outward life that we and others see. Our outer lives are a reflection of our inner lives. We live out what we see and hear in our heads. It is in becoming aware of the inner environment that we empower ourselves to change the outer environment.

Okay, so you get that if you change your mind, you change your life—right? I wish it were that easy. I wish all I had to do was tell myself to think positively and say some affirmations and—poof—all my dreams would come true. Do not misunderstand what I am suggesting here. I am saying that sometimes it takes work on a deeper level to make the adjustments necessary to succeed; it is a process of redefining yourself. We all have a stream of thought running through our minds at all times. Scientists have demonstrated that there is brain activity even when we sleep.

We draw self-definition from before the time we were born. There is evidence that babies are influenced in the womb. This makes sense, because the mother releases molecules into her bloodstream when she has a mood change. The baby feels this.

When I was in graduate school, the question of nature (genetics) versus nurture (environment) was discussed. I was, and still am, of the belief that both have an influence, as some research indicates. My point here is that who you have decided to be today is influenced not only by the genes you carry, but also by the environment you were raised in and the environment you have created.

Begin changing what you are choosing to believe about yourself. Take the uncomfortable steps toward what you want, and watch as your outer environment begins to change. Think about the thoughts that enter your field of consciousness, as there is a constant stream of thought. This is the self-messaging that you do on a regular basis. For example:

> "I am beautiful."
> "I am fat."
> "I am no good at finances."
> "I can't be a millionaire because …"
> "I'm not as good as the successful person sitting next to me."

And the inner dialogue goes on and on. This stream of thought is part of defining who you are in the moment. Your outer environment is defined by it because it keeps you from taking the steps necessary to be where you want to be in life and business.

Be willing to redefine yourself as you go. Other people around you may disapprove of your new definitions; let that be okay. Remember that they may be as uncomfortable with the new you as you are. Some people simply will not be able to continue their relationship with you as it was previously. When you live with integrity and by your standards—*genuinely*—it brings to light where others are not doing so, and that is not always pleasant to look at. This can bring friendships (or what appeared to be friendships) to an end. Say a blessing as they go.

> "Being a fool is an indictment of arrogance and stupidity."
> —Johnny Faulkner

Chapter 3

🌿 EDUCATION AND CRITICAL THINKING

For some, the word "critical" has a negative connotation. However, in today's world, an ability to think critically is necessary for our well being. To further define critical thinking, it is an ability to think independently, or for yourself. It is exercising the ability to decide whether something or someone is good for you, and not just taking another's word for it.

You probably use your critical thinking skills when you hear or see ads on radio and television. Advertisements can be elusive and leave the critical thinker perplexed. Weight-loss commercials are particularly amusing. Pay attention to what words are used and the objects or people seen in them, for there are always subtle messages. I recently saw an ad for a weight-loss program for men, but the camera panned over to the abdomen of a young woman in a bikini. Hmm. What does that have to do with weight loss for men? More sex maybe? I have heard that sex sells.

Whenever you are creating change in your life, education—such as reading this book—is necessary. You have to decide whether the information in this book is useful and based on what you believe and find is true. Any information that is disseminated should be treated that way. However, what I have noticed is that the media can put out misinformation and the general public will buy it. And if someone with enough letters following his or her name puts it out there, it must be the gospel truth!

One example that comes to mind is a news report aired on television and printed in the *New York Times* in January 2007 that stated 51 percent of American women live without husbands and portrayed a less-than-favorable picture of marriage. What was not stated was that the "women" in the census numbers used for the article were as young as 15 years of age. I would hope that these young women prefer to be single at that age! They still have much growing up to do, as well as learning about themselves and the world around them. Another group of women included in the census were military wives whose husbands are deployed in Iraq. Need I say anything about this category? I ask myself what this has to do with the category of single, marriageable-age women. I don't understand the motive behind such a story other than that perhaps someone had an agenda. I call it irresponsible reporting, as the subjects did not seem qualified for the study.

Look more deeply at the information provided to you. Decide if you wish to buy into it. Remember, you are developing beliefs based on information. What if the information is wrong? How do you know that you are reading or hearing the truth? That is tricky. You can always find a plethora of information and varying opinions on the internet about almost *anything*. Ask what others have learned regarding whatever subject you are inquiring about. The truth is out there; we simply have to be willing to seek it out.

Chapter 4

BE A STUDENT

If your health or financial picture is not optimal, it is up to you to take the time to educate yourself about the changes you need to make for optimal results. Some people just want to believe what they read in popular magazines and see in television ads or programs. They don't take into account that sensationalism sells or do any research to find out the facts. If you are not willing to become a student of your own life, how do you ever expect to learn and make deep, sustainable changes? Set aside 20 minutes per day to focus on learning about money management, the psychology around money, health issues, marital issues, or whatever subject matter pertains to the change you want to see in your life. If your marriage is in the garbage can of life, reading the latest article in a magazine is not going to fix the issue. Watching some of the drama-ridden shows on television will not help, either. Find credible sources to feed your mind. If you are unwilling to change who you are "being," what do you expect to accomplish with a bunch of "doing" (i.e., activity)? Chances are, your "doing" will be determined by who you are "being."

How do you know if the package of "Tasty, Healthy Butter Stuff" in your refrigerator is healthy for you? Do you take the package's word for it? Do you believe the actor dressed up like a doctor on the television commercial? Or do you look at the ingredient list and decide for yourself? The burden of responsibility falls on your shoulders. Understand that advertisements and packaging have one goal: selling you their product. Look back over time and notice how many times food items have first been deemed healthy and then unhealthy for consumption. Drugs go through the same cycles. Claims usually begin with the words, "The latest research shows...." Check out the research! Who is telling you this stuff? Who did the research: the competitor, the one promoting the new and better product, or an objective group that is not being funded by a group with an agenda? It is up to you to exercise critical thinking skills and responsibility.

Here is a news flash: eating fast food in large quantities can be detrimental to your health and wellness. Check it out! My point is, challenge the information you receive. Don't take my word about this information. Look for yourself. Think for yourself. Look more deeply. You create your reality in each and every moment. You must be responsible for your well being and what you choose to believe. An advanced degree is not a guarantee of truth or quality. Taking just a little time to learn more about the decisions you are making could save you a lot of time, energy, heartache, and money. Educate yourself and be vigilant about what you choose to build belief structures on. Create your day! Create your life! What do you choose right now?

Chapter 5

ATTRACTION, OR LIVING IN GOD SPACE

There are many books, videos, and seminars available about the law of attraction. This is a generic term. What is the law of attraction? How do you use it? Is it truly a concept of "what you think about, you bring about?" This may sound a little airy-fairy to logical thinkers.

I am compelled to rename this dynamic, as so many struggle with its origin and delivery methods. Lack of scientific data also renders this theory unfounded. I think a more accurate name is living in God Space.

There are individuals who claim to have used the attraction principles to gain health, wealth, and abundance. In the time of Jesus, miraculous claims were made, and many scoffed them. We have miracles occurring every day all around us, and many disbelieve them.

Some camps would label this the work of the devil. Why must this be the work of the devil or New Age thought? To be a good Christian, do I need to be broke and celibate with horrible events in my life? Where does the Bible tell us to live miserably in order to be holy?

The logical thinker might say it is only coincidence that great and miraculous things happen. Luck is another common term for this. Talk about a joy stealer. I want to know that I am the cocaptain of my ship!

God Space is the energy that we never see. I use the term energy because this is how I can best comprehend the dynamic at play. God moves through and around us; he is everything, as he is the creator. Since God is the great "I am," it stands to reason that life is occurring in God Space. Since God created this universe as we know it, then it must be running like a well-oiled machine, because he doesn't make mistakes. How does a coincidence occur in that case? At times, we have unexplainable events in our lives. Things happen occasionally that make us think or say, "No way, I can't believe this happened!"

God's law of how things transpire is set. We have free will to live and move about in that law as we choose. We can hang ourselves (metaphorically speaking), or we can live joyously and abundantly. We choose how we respond to events. Some ask how a nonbeliever can prosper. Again, the law of how things operate is set. It is a choice about how to move in that energy. Ultimately, we have to answer for our choices in the end.

Jesus broke laws of science, medicine, religion, and governing men. The miracles he performed were and still are unexplainable by scientific standards. I think the law of attraction title poses a challenge to the thinking of so many because of how God has been somewhat removed from this theory by some sources. Or perhaps it sounds too good to be true. It is not addressed as such in the Bible; blessings and miracles might be more appropriate terms to illustrate the dynamic.

When I break down the law of attraction as I view it and use it, it is simple and looks something like this:

1. Be clear about your intention
2. Think optimally
3. Focus on your destination
4. Believe and have faith
5. Persevere
6. Celebrate along the way
7. Give thanks

How do the above points differ from the way Jesus appears to have lived? That is all that living in God Space or the law of attraction poses to us.

Some material available in the form of movies, books, CD's and so on may not resonate with you 100 percent of the time, but they still contain some good messages. I was once told, "When you eat fish, do you eat the bones? Do you not eat fish because it has bones? You have to be willing to discard what doesn't work for you." I couldn't agree more. Be responsible and use your critical thinking skills.

Speaking of responsibility, sometimes I get the impression that some think God is sitting on a throne in the clouds and, for daily entertainment, points his scepter at particular individuals and manipulates their lives like pawns on a chessboard. You will hear this from some who are angry with

God for one reason or another and those who struggle with the concept of God. Others use this line of reasoning to avoid taking responsibility for their lives. Perhaps an obstacle appears in their path, and they stop with the belief that God doesn't want them to do this or that.

God Space is operating all the time, whether you are aware of it or not. Maybe you are aware of it and wish to change who and what keeps showing up in your life. If you are ready to begin the process of change and living in God Space, the journey begins with the awareness of your internal dynamics that need to change.

Chapter 6

LIKE ATTRACTS LIKE: GOD SPACE UP CLOSE

It is a miracle that the human body does what it does on a moment-to-moment basis. Our bodies are made up of multiple systems that are, in turn, made up of various groupings of cells. If you look at the cellular level of the body, according to work done by Dr. Candace Pert, receptor sites can be found there. These receptors are programmed to pick up molecules of a certain energy-resonance pattern or vibration. When we have thought and emotional state changes, the molecules in our body change. Our cells pick up the various molecules through receptor sites, and we have feeling changes, meaning an energy-resonance or vibration-pattern change has occurred. Think about a time when you were happy or sad. Where do you feel happy or sad? The whole body is affected.

Try this exercise: Think about being around someone who absolutely drains you, then think about being with someone who is fun and uplifting to be with. Pay attention to your body as you visualize this. Who would you rather spend time with? Why? What is the difference? *They are operating at different energy frequencies.*

Medical science uses high-frequency ultrasound waves to break up kidney stones. Radio-wave ablation is used to disrupt or destroy heart muscle tissue that is thought to cause abnormal heart rhythms. The human body responds to various energy frequencies, because various energy frequencies exist in the body.

Consider the fun and uplifting person you thought of in the above exercise. Does he or she hang around with depressing and drama-ridden people much of the time? Probably not.

If an individual walks around focused on how the world is doing him or her wrong and believes that people are jerks, then that person is operating in that energy frequency. Guess what shows up consistently? It is almost as if this type of individual is looking to gather evidence to support that thinking pattern. It is amazing how something is always happening in that person's life to bring him or her down. It's like Rosanne Rosannadanna, on *Saturday Night Live,* used to say: "It's always something."

The Swiss psychologist Carl Jung developed the theory of synchronicity. Basically, his theory states that we manifest the things we think about. Others call this meaningful coincidence, miracles, and blessings. Whatever you call it, you think about something and then it manifests in your life. Do not be misled by this simple statement. It often takes more than just having a thought about something or someone to manifest. I mean, if you could win the lottery simply by thinking about it, then the lottery would be bankrupt!

I don't believe that the theory of synchronicity has been scientifically proven. The theory of synchronicity is one way to look at God Space, as I define it. How do you describe how miracles come about? Do we know how Jesus performed miracles? The obvious answer is through the power of God. However, the movement of that power or energy is what I am talking about. That is, the activity that occurs in that space between the individual with the intention and the manifestation of the miracle or blessing itself. We don't have scientific data to explain that.

Synchronicities, blessings, and miracles happen every day. We just have to look for them. No manifestation is too small or too large. Who is to deem your miracle too inconsequential? Of the many ways God has moved in my life, one memorable event for me was when I was going through my divorce and wanted to go back to school. I spent much time focused on, and talking to others about, going back to school. I took the steps necessary to apply for financial assistance, but did not know if I could afford to go to school.

As I was driving home from work one day, I was thinking about strategies to get into school. At the time, I was not making much money and was a single parent. When I arrived home, I checked the mail. There was a letter stating that I had been awarded a Pell Grant to attend school that year. Wow, free schooling! Talk about a blessing (or synchronicity).

A more recent example is dear to my heart. I began stating that I was ready to have horses. I shared this with my husband and knew that I was in a place in life to embrace this experience. I had a lot of energy flowing into this thought, as it was so exciting for me. I spent time envisioning myself on a horse and horses in our pasture. About 10 days later, a former client phoned. As we were chatting, I mentioned that I was looking for a larger vehicle to haul horses. In the course of the conversation, my client became excited because she was looking for an appropriate owner for her horses. She was not willing to let them go to just anyone. They are now in their new home, and are an exceptional match for my husband and me. It was that easy—no going from pony to pony and test driving each one. The perfect horses showed up. I began verbalizing the desire for horses, and it took only 10 days for them to appear. When we choose to let God do his work, we are connected to the right people to experience the blessings and miracles.

Another example is much smaller, but great nonetheless. Because my body shape had changed (meaning I needed the next larger size), I spent an entire Saturday afternoon searching local department stores for the right pair of jeans. I found the perfect-fitting pair, but the price tag was not perfect for my budget. I agreed with myself as I left the store without the jeans that I would wait for a sale and get them at a lower price. Two weeks later, I was driving around and saw a garage sale. I love to treasure hunt at garage sales. I popped in and saw a pile of jeans on a table—the very jeans I had seen at the department store. They were my size, and I got five pairs for 25 dollars, a savings of 300 dollars over the department store price. That is what I call a sale and a wonderful blessing (or synchronicity).

As you go through your day, take note of the synchronicities, blessings, and miracles that occur. You may think of someone you haven't seen since high school and then you'll run into him or her at the grocery store. You may focus on a goal consistently and take steps every day toward that goal. People and events will begin to show up out of seemingly nowhere to support you on the journey to your goal.

As you move through your 90-day journey, allow yourself to be stretched and challenged. Be willing to get out of your self-imposed box and take even a baby step in the direction of your goal. Remember, there is no failure. Some say, "Fail forward." Just use it as an opportunity to learn and do it differently next time. It is an awakening to God's movement in your life. Have faith and allow Him to unfold the path before you so that you may flow along the path to success.

I like the way God Space works. It is a lot of fun, and it happens when I least expect it. I love a good adventure. Perhaps one day we will have a better understanding of the unexplainable. Until then, we have to walk in faith.

Bible Passage: Philippians 2:13

If you want blessings and abundance, be that blessing to others.

Chapter 7

ATTITUDES OF INERTIA

There truly is a thought process and behavioral pattern that supports health, wellness, and abundance. I mention health, wellness, and abundance because there is a correlation. As I mentioned previously, we choose what energy frequency we want to operate at. For example, we can choose to focus on a happy and healthier attitude, or we can choose to focus on misery. Rest assured that the behavior will follow the attitude. Perhaps you have heard the Be—Do—Have statement. *Be* who you need to be so that you can *do* what you need to do to *have* what you want to have. This statement has been around for quite some time; I am only repeating it here as it is a great summary.

As a coach and counselor, I have worked with many in the arena of attraction and have encountered many different attitudes about the subject. Three common attitudes I have noticed that get in the way of attracting health, wellness, and abundance are magical thinking, the time-deficit paradox, and immobilization.

Magical thinking is a term commonly found in psychology textbooks. It is an attitude that all you need is some daily affirmations or other daily ritual, and your wildest dreams will come true. You might as well sit in a corner and throw some salt over your shoulder. The outcome is likely to be the same. Now, do not misunderstand me; I believe in and advocate that solid affirmations are a necessary ingredient in making the transition into the flow of attraction, health, and wellness, but there is more involved than mindlessly reciting some affirmations.

In the *time-deficit paradox,* people do not want to take the time to explore where they hold themselves back and make the necessary thought and behavioral pattern changes needed to live life on their new terms. This takes time and energy, something that some are not willing to invest in themselves. They are caught up in the idea of "busyness." They have not yet grasped that less is more. They think they just need to do more. Did you notice the word "do" in there? Where is "be"? If what you have been thinking and doing is not working, then why repeat it and expect a different outcome? This person may think, "If I could just do _____, then I could be _____. That is working in reverse, which has proved to be counterproductive. If I fill in the blanks with "marathon" and "physically fit," does it make sense? Considering that a marathon is about 26 miles long, I think we can all agree that you need to *be* in good physical condition before *doing* a marathon.

Immobilized people know what changes need to be made and simply choose not to do them. They are well aware of their dissatisfaction with life or business and still keep on doing things and thinking in the same patterns that do not work. At first glance, this doesn't make sense. Look more deeply at what is really going on. There is resistance to the changes. Sometimes it is simply fear: if I change who I am being, what does this mean? The victimhood mentality is often at play here, and some boundaries need to be set. To a person with this mindset, it is easier to allow another to determine his or her destiny. Others feel unclear about the steps necessary to making change and need outside support. These people must learn to trust themselves and begin to build confidence in taking action toward whatever they want.

Chapter 8

YOUR HEALTH: DON'T BE A LEMMING

The human body is a miracle, and there is still so much we don't know. I think we will look back in 100 years and view today's medicine as somewhat barbaric. In order to progress, the concept of the magic bullet pill has to be overcome. What I mean by the magic bullet pill is the idea that the human body can just be treated like trash. That is, we put into it all the processed food, supplements, pharmaceuticals, and any other substance imaginable. Then, when the body breaks down (yet again), the doctor can fix it with a pill. We have to move beyond this pharmaceutical panacea idea. I have been guilty of this mentality myself. The sooner we take responsibility about pharmaceuticals and food (as well as other substances), the sooner health will be restored to many.

That last statement may be a little strong, and I am not suggesting that people quit taking their medications, because sometimes they are necessary. I am suggesting that people become more responsible about taking or prescribing a cocktail of medications.

I know that physicians are busy people. Who has time to sit down and research all the drugs and their interactions with each other? However, I am not comfortable knowing that the general public is the testing ground for the madness of medicine. Some may point out that the Food and Drug Administration exists to stop anything harmful. I am not convinced that there is enough work done in the area of drugs interacting with one another nor am I convinced that drugs are properly tested, period. I wonder how many drugs have expedited a person's death and it goes unnoticed because the cause of death seemed unrelated. Where is the FDA in that?

What keeps more and more physicians from looking into the root cause of the illnesses they see? Isn't it kind of weird that all of these new problems and illnesses are cropping up? Does anyone care, or is the doctor just glad to see me come through the office door and charge me for the office visit and procedures performed? I know the pharmaceutical company is glad to see me pick up my prescriptions!

When birth control pills first came out, many complications occurred (that is putting it mildly). I am not convinced that "the pill" is a good thing today. Antidepressants are handed out like candy now. Physicians with little or no education in psychology as I understand it are prescribing mood-altering drugs. Do they think that a mood-altering drug is going to fix the problem underlying the depressed mood? Did the patient become depressed because his or her blood levels of Zoloft or some other Selective Serotonin Reuptake Inhibitor (SSRI) fell too low? The use of antidepressants in children is also another concern that Dr. Joseph Glenmullen addresses in his book *The Antidepressant Solution*. I like how Dr. William Glasser views depression. He says it is not a noun, it is a verb. That is, the individual is not depressed, he or she is *depressing* something. In my own experience, both personally and professionally, I have found that depression not only stems from an event being depressed, but also, more often than not, is accompanied by a physiological event.

I experienced depression and anxiety when my body began to malfunction. Now granted, I had buried two very dear people in my life after watching them waste away to nothing due to cancer. Yes, there was a life event coinciding with my depression and anxiety. However, after taking an SSRI over a period of time, I took a nosedive health-wise. I gained a marked amount of weight, couldn't sleep at night, and couldn't stay awake during the day. I had mood swings and lost the ability to focus. I began having unexplainable skin rashes and chronic yeast infections everywhere. My hair thinned and I could not get warm or stay that way in the winter, even though I remained in front of the fire much of the time. I won't depress you with any more of this experience; let's just say that I was miserable. Looking back, my clients felt better than I did, and I had to compensate for this as best as I could. I would catnap between appointments because I couldn't stay awake, mostly because I wasn't getting quality sleep at night. Many around me said they would not have known I was feeling so bad. It's amazing how we learn to compensate and mask our feelings. I also felt that it served no one to wallow in misery. Somehow, I managed to Tony Robbins myself through each day.

I went to the doctor, who tested my thyroid and determined that it was functioning in what was considered a "normal" range. I left thinking that it was just the depression getting to me. We also came to the conclusion that a prescription was needed for the yeast problem.

There were a few things overlooked by all involved. One was that the thyroid test may reflect "normal" based on a statistical average, but it was not normal for me. Another was a protocol for someone with a yeast overgrowth as bad as mine was. And finally, the years of birth-control pills had taken a toll on me, with estrogen dominance. So, all of this together was literally killing me. It was definitely killing my marriage, because I was grumpy much of the time and my libido was nonexistent. I often wonder how many marriages are affected by such health issues.

I could have resigned myself to the thought that I was going to be one of those incapacitated, depressed people and be miserable the rest of my life, *or* I could keep searching for answers. This was not *me*. I am energetic and happy. I chose to keep searching, and found a doctor who helped me on the journey to recovering my health.

It has been a journey, and I continue to move more and more into a healthy balance. It did not happen overnight with a magic bullet pill, either. Granted, when I began the journey, there were some awesome results quickly, but not a restoration of full and balanced health as I now perceive it. That took a little time to re-establish.

My point in sharing my story is that you have to take responsibility for your health. You cannot trust a person simply because he or she has a medical degree. Be critical and do research before taking prescription drugs. Look at possible side effects; how will the new drug interact with the drug(s) you're currently taking? Look at how long the drug has been out. Do you want to be in the first group of lemmings? Ask yourself if you are taking a pill to squelch a symptom or if the pill gets to the root of the problem.

Understand that physicians get much of their information from the pharmaceutical companies. The pharmaceutical industry is a trillion-dollar business. Powerful! I have heard through the grapevine that some believe the industry would have to keep the cure for cancer under wraps if they found it, because they fear the consequences of releasing the cure. This sounds ludicrous, but think of the lost revenue if everyone was healthy. Another point to ponder is that when a drug trial is performed, if anyone responds favorably to the placebo, those people are omitted from the study. Why not put some energy into studying that miracle? Do you read or hear about that in the brochures, websites, or television commercials? In *The Biology of Belief,* Dr. Bruce Lipton mentions this and how the hype about the effectiveness of antidepressants in the media has actually improved their effectiveness in clinical trials. He also points out instances where the power of the mind healed the body. The mind can override the body and heal it. You can find a number of cases. Neil McHugh takes the reader through his journey of healing using the power of his mind in *Dreaming Your Way To Pain-Free Living*.

When I look at the big picture, it is frightening. It seems that pharmaceutical companies are interested in squelching symptoms. If you become healthy, what revenue can be gained from that?

I sometimes wonder if there is not a mindset that looks for a new group of symptoms to create the next new diagnosis and then develop a drug to squelch the symptoms. A wonderful television commercial would then be developed to let people know that they are suffering from something like "hyper thumb syndrome." And the masses would flock to their local physicians to get the new drug because who wants to suffer with a hyper thumb?

The pharmaceutical companies offer seminars and have representatives going from office to office leaving information, informing doctors about the latest and greatest drug. What happened to balancing the body and actually healing the body? There is an episode of the television sitcom *Scrubs* that beautifully illustrates this dynamic. Heather Locklear portrays a pharmaceutical representative who feeds the doctors a steak dinner and tantalizes them in a sexual manner. Dr. Kelso buys right into the idea of the new drug, and Dr. Cox portrays more of my attitude on this matter: he realizes the seduction at work.

Here is the good news about disease: much of it is preventable if the individual is willing to be responsible and do a little work. The body is a grouping of smaller systems working in harmony. When one system is out of balance, it stands to reason that the other systems are affected. Look at how long our grandparents lived. Many were farmers and ate food they grew or others grew. They ate real butter, fresh eggs, milk, meat, and vegetables when in season. We do not eat that way much anymore. The food we have available now has come from a more mineral-deficient soil and is loaded with preservatives and additives.

Look at the plight we have with diseases. Some argue that we are living longer now. And what is the quality of life of those living longer? Are they in nursing homes being kept alive with modern medicine and not even cognizant of their surroundings? Is that a quality life? I am not here to argue the ethics of life and death. I am hoping to point out that modern medicine is not necessarily keeping us on the golf course until we are 90 years old. You must decide how much responsibility you are willing to take in your destiny.

I have provided references for your viewing pleasure at the back of this book. Take up a new hobby, reading, if you haven't already. It could save your life or the life of a loved one. Many books are now on CD—listen to them! Don't be a lemming and just follow the masses to the pharmacy for your magic bullet pill.

Chapter 9

🌿 YOUR WEALTH: MANIFESTED ENERGY

There are certain subjects that Americans generally don't seem to feel comfortable discussing. Sex and relationships (in a healthy manner), death, and money are at the top of that list. We are taught many things in school at all levels, but we do not get an education about how to treat money. We have the opportunity in many schools to get basic sex education, but not education about relationships. We do not get education or preparation to handle death, either our own or someone else's. These are the most important aspects of our lives. I think all high schools need to have a class called "Real Life" with a curriculum on death (we all die), relationships (most of us have one), and money (gotta have it!).

I am going to address money here only briefly. Money is nothing more than energy manifested. Think about it. That money in your wallet is nothing more than paper and ink or pressed metal of some sort. The only reason it holds value is because you give it value. It is exchanged for goods and services. You have received money for your goods or services if you did not win the lottery, steal, or inherit the money.

There are varying attitudes about money. Some feel that money is the root of all evil and think that wealthy people have gained their money at the expense of others. This gives an inanimate object (money) much power. It is the intention of the person behind the money that brings evil into the picture. Some people have always struggled to gain money and don't know how to do otherwise. Others appear to amass money easily and embrace abundance. Your financial picture reflects how you think about money and ultimately yourself. This is what is so scary. Where do most of us learn to manage or mismanage our money? From the two people that we spent most of our time with—our parents. Look at the attitudes your parents hold toward money. Are yours similar or have you thrown out what you learned? I am not suggesting that we all turn and point a finger at our parents. We are all grownups now and must take responsibility for our own attitudes and actions. I note this only so that you will be vigilant about who you listen to in the future. You do not want to assimilate the belief systems of those who seem to struggle.

One belief system that is fairly common is that God wants us to live like paupers. If that is the case, why did he give Adam and Eve the Garden of Eden? One might argue that the ensuing behavior on the part of Adam and Eve is why we must live in struggle, but mankind was not cursed to live in poverty. Our growth and expansion is a credit to God. Lives are changed with the expansion and growth of mankind. I speak of growth in a healthy manner. We can make a difference in the world with our own growth and expansion. We have a God of abundance.

We can't help others rise above their scarcity by joining them. We can help them by expanding beyond the fear and scarcity. Be the example, and put pictures of abundance into their heads. They will benefit greatly from this, provided they are willing to grow. If you look at the welfare system in this country, it is not hard to see how we (yes, we) have created a monster. Through reinforcement of money energy, many have developed a mindset that their welfare check is their paycheck. One has to wonder why we even have an unemployment rate in this country, but that is subject matter for another book.

The scarcity of money can captivate attention and monopolize much time and energy. I can explain this a little better using a model developed by the humanistic psychologist Abraham Maslow, who developed the Hierarchy of Needs. This theory points out that a person's focus remains on the level of needs that are not met. The levels, or hierarchy, are:

Self-Actualization

Esteem

Love/Belonging

Safety

Physiological

If the most basic (physiological) needs on the bottom rung are not met, then the focus stays there in an attempt to get them met. For instance, if you don't have a home or food readily available, you will spend much of your time and energy seeking food and shelter. Once those needs are met, your attention can then move on up the hierarchy. When a health crisis occurs, your focus is on finding health. As you move up into love and belonging, emotional needs crop up. You may have an unmet need to feel loved to the point of sacrificing your own needs or safety to get it met. An example of this might be having unprotected sex in an attempt to feel loved or accepted. Another example is getting involved in, and for whatever reason staying in, an obviously abusive relationship. As you move up the ladder, and needs are met at the lower levels, the focus begins to turn to creativity and problem solving in the self-actualization level. This can cause much introspection as you begin to become aware of where your attention or focus is much of the time. What needs are you working on getting met? Think about what captures your attention much of the time. A professional coach or counselor can assist you in working through unmet needs if you feel stuck in one area.

Take a moment to review your attitude toward your money. If money were your friend, how would your friend be feeling about your relationship right now, based on how you treat it? The energy of money responds to your attitude toward it. Looking for ways to get rid of it is not accumulating and amassing it. Seek methods to accumulate it, and let money work for you, instead of you working for it. Let it multiply.

Chapter 10

RESPONSIBILITY, OR THE LACK THEREOF

Americans live in a litigious society. Sometimes it feels like we are a country of "It's not my fault," or a country of victimhood. I see diet pill commercials on television that tell you it's not your fault that you are overweight. I guess it is the fault of the fast-food chains for supersizing your order, or perhaps your car's fault for driving you through and ordering. I have not quite figured out what they mean by telling you it's not your fault and that yet another pill will fix everything. I am aware of medical conditions that contribute to body weight issues, but there are folks out there who are unwilling to take responsibility for their health, among other things. I am not just picking on the diet industry, although obesity is a big problem in this country. This applies to many facets of life. Look anywhere there is blame going around. There is always a level of responsibility-dodging going on. Why do we need fault anyway?

What happens if we remove fault and judgment from this picture? It is what it is. You may not be happy or feel healthy with where your body is right now or where your life and career is. Where do you want to be? What does it take to get there? The question is, "Are you willing and committed to taking the steps toward what you want?" Is there an area that you can identify where you drop the ball? If so, what support systems need to be put in place to support growth in that area? What needs to change to have this be different for you?

You can do anything you set your mind to. A little help along the way may be the necessary ingredient to get you there. Whenever you are addressing change in your life, you are assuming responsibility for your life. You may experience issues with money, time, energy, or health. If there are areas that you are not happy with, you have a choice. Standing around whining about it is not going to change the situation.

Set aside time each day to educate yourself about the area in which you would like to see change. If your business isn't going the way you would like it to, where can you find information on changing it? There are books and magazines on every subject imaginable. If you don't believe me, check out the bookstores. If you are not willing to embrace change, when will enough be enough?

Chapter 11

BLAME, JUDGMENT, AND OTHER DANCES IN VICTIMHOOD

Judgment is perhaps the most elusive of human conditions. We all make judgments throughout the day: I like this, I don't like that, some of those are okay, that won't work, and this will work. Typically, when we think of judgment, we think of having an opinion, making an accusation, or having a belief about another individual. We can also pass judgment on ourselves. Anytime we compare ourselves to others and find that we do or don't measure up, we are passing judgment on self. This turns into the negative mental undertow that I discuss in a later chapter. This is a sneaky and vicious thing that you can get caught up in. I invite you to stop any self-defeating or self-sabotaging thinking and behavioral patterns that you may have now. If you constantly tell yourself that you do not measure up to whomever or whatever, you never will measure up. You will see only what you choose to focus on. Notice the false personal belief in here? Remember my statement about being a creation of God and that he doesn't make mistakes? What will it take for you to put on blinders, focus on what you want, and run the race without looking at the person next to you to see if you are measuring up?

Judgment passed on others is common, too. This often falls under the heading of blame, which leads us down the road to victimhood. Whenever we feel powerless, we can point the finger at someone else and stop owning our role in the drama that is unfolding. Blaming another gives power to another person, power that he or she does not truly possess. If you are unhappy and blame another for being unhappy, do you see that you are allowing an external source determine your mood? Wow, now that is power! Happiness is an inside job!

When someone feels small, he or she may try to push others down or make them wrong. This allows him or her the illusion of feeling bigger. This is the blame game in action: to create a victimizer so we can all feel victimized and sorry for one another.

Are you blaming any of your emotional states on another? Are you blaming any of your circumstances on others? I see this in the business world when one person is blaming others in general for the company not being where the person would like it to be. Who is running that business? Who is making the decisions about day-to-day activities in that business? Whenever you catch yourself pointing a finger, examine your role in the situation. You may have an "ouch" moment, but it is an opportunity for change and growth.

Chapter 12

FILLING IN THE GAPS IN LIFE

Many people hold onto habits that no longer serve them. Although they are aware that they hold on to them, they are often not clear about why they do. In this case, the *why* can help change the habit. When I mention "habits," I am talking about activities done habitually, like compulsive shopping, being in bad relationships, watching pornography, video gaming and even substance use/abuse.

What is going on? Take a step back and look at the dynamic. If people spend their alone time making purchases, they may be filling the empty space in their lives with "stuff." The problem here is that it does not truly fulfill the need. (Refer back to Maslow's hierarchy of needs, page 42.) They wake up the next day wondering, "What have I done?" If you have ever drunk too much alcohol, you may have woken up the next day with the same thought.

The bad-relationship dynamic is the same. Some people stay in a relationship that they are fully aware is not good for them, but it fills the void in their life with a warm body. They fear being alone and cannot fathom getting rid of the unhealthy relationship, because they are convinced that there is no one better out there. The paradox is that being alone and unhappy is easier than having the aggravation of the other person in the bad relationship and being unhappy. I see individuals justify and deny their bad relationships. They list the bad behavior and annoyances of their bad relationship, and in the same breath talk about how wonderful the other person makes them feel. Put on your magnifying glasses and note the last three words in the last sentence: "makes them feel." *Wow*—those are powerful people. The bad relationship person "makes them feel" good. That is powerful, when you consider that no other human being truly has power over how you think and feel.

Another way to fill in the gaps in life is through the internet. It has really made the world seem smaller. We can communicate with someone literally on the opposite side of the planet in seconds. It is a wonderful portal to gain information and communicate. Psychotherapy is delivered in virtual reality now, with reports of success. It can create a safe space for the participant.

The internet also brings undesirable aspects with it. Video games and pornography can take the place of actual human interaction. These are dynamics that hook people in, and the internet replaces actual human contact and interaction. It allows the individual to replace social interaction with what appears to be a safe and distant interactive dynamic. In the case of pornography, some feel that they are not actually cheating on their significant other by participating in internet porn, but mentally the deed has been done. In *Think Before You Look,* Daniel Henderson describes the impact that pornography has on the individual as well as on society as a whole.

Video game addiction is beginning to get some press, especially with some games being correlated with school shootings. It seems to captivate the younger crowd and pull them away from more physical and interactive games. This can affect overall health because of a decline in physical activity.

Substance use and abuse is a way of medicating the pain and voids in life. People use drugs to numb themselves or try to fill emptiness. I also see food used this way, such as when people eat to shove down the pain. When they become anxious, they reach for food, drugs, alcohol, or some other substance.

I wish there was a way to convey that the emptiness can be filled in more healthy and joyful ways; however, that is easier said than done. There are many programs and tools out there to help fill in the gaps and support healing.

Many individuals think, "I should be able to handle my own problems." Really? Why "should" you be able to and—more important—why aren't you? If you or people you know are carrying around a heavy bag of pain, hurt, emptiness, substance abuse, compulsive eating, or spending, or any other habit that isn't serving them or their loved ones, take a look at it! Have you been withholding the truth from them or yourself? Do you fear losing their friendship if you say, "Hey, I love you but I think there's a problem here?" Do you fear losing friends if you admit to having a problem? If you admit to struggling with something and people in your life go away, that's *great.* They weren't friends to begin with, and you need to find some new ones, anyway.

Some view counseling or psychotherapy as admitting that they are "broken" or that there is something wrong with them. The truth is ,if your life isn't working—get some help. We all can use professional counseling at one point in life or another. Counseling is like having a confidante whom you can open up to and be real with. A counselor is there to be your sounding board as well as help you put the pieces together. His or her job is to listen deeply to you and give you feedback in a way that supports your growth and confidence. What is wrong with getting your life to work? I suppose you look more together now with your life not working? Have you not suffered enough? I have met people who seem to enjoy the pain of their lives not working. They roll in pain like a pig in mud; there is definitely a payoff for staying in the mud hole. Take your power back! Happiness is an inside job!

Matthew 5: 27–28

Chapter 13

EMOTIONAL BONDAGE VS. EMOTIONAL INTEGRITY

Another thing that contributes to mental and physical well-being is emotional integrity. Emotional integrity is being truthful with yourself and others about how you feel in the moment or about a situation. Sometimes, we find ourselves in awkward situations and grasping for words or stumbling around in our own mind trying to figure out what we feel. Awareness of the confusion and fear in any situation is the first step. Clarity has to be gained about the feelings that are rolling around in your mind.

Start by writing all your thoughts and feelings down on paper, or speak them aloud. The ability to be emotionally honest with yourself and others can serve you well. If you are hurt or angry, express it in a healthy way. That can be as simple as saying, "I feel angry (or hurt) whenever I hear (or experience) _____." Some learn, over time, to simply abandon themselves. What I mean by this is, they internalize their hurt or anger. We can learn to do this very early in life. For instance, if we spoke our truth to another, probably a loved one, and either the person went away or punished us, we would then make the connection that saying how we feel results in being abandoned or punished. This can be a painful process, and the pattern of avoiding the truth begins. In other words, we get out of integrity with our emotional self. We can even begin to take responsibility for how others feel and begin a dance to "make them feel" (one way or another) or dance so that they don't feel one way or another. For example, you might withhold telling someone how he or she is hurting you because you don't want to hurt or anger that person.

You do not hold the power to make people feel or think anything. They do that all on their own. Let them own their feelings. God is not on vacation.

Many times, a boundary is all that needs to be drawn to effectively express yourself. Boundaries are meant to be loving and gentle, not hateful and hurtful. My recommendation here is to read *Boundaries* by Dr. Henry Cloud and Dr. John Townsend.

Holding in emotional responses is unhealthy. It can cause the release of detrimental chemicals in your body, which over time wears down the immune system and can contribute to disease and illness. You can find plenty of literature about how stress contributes to illness.

Holding in your feelings affects who and what is showing up in your life. For example, let's say that a man has held in much anger over his lifetime. He encounters people and situations that tap anger issues with him. Perhaps he encounters rude people much of the time or ends up in situations that anger him further. He probably looks angry much of the time as well. This man can end up with heart problems, elevated blood pressure, symptoms of depression, or a myriad of other health problems.

The person who always puts on a happy face but is miserable on the inside encounters difficulties as well. Look at the discrepancy here. Putting on a happy face and ignoring the elephant in the living room is not handling the problem.

Another aspect of this is unforgiveness. What I mean by this is the dynamic of holding onto a past hurt, and not forgiving yourself or another for a transgression. Some walk around in this state all their lives. Unforgiveness holds us in the past. We do not move forward because we are locked in the past with an emotional tie. It becomes a holding pattern in the past.

Forgiveness is a process and can become a daily pursuit in some situations, especially when loved ones are involved. The important thing to note is that releasing past transgressions allows you to raise your energy and move forward, feeling much lighter along the way. I know this may be easier said than done, but it is possible to do so with ease, grace, and joy. Use of the Three Rs (Chapter 18), especially the release step, can be helpful in forgiveness.

Unresolved issues also hold you in the past. Perhaps you had a fight with a friend or relative that was swept under the rug, or an instance where you did not speak your truth or stand up for what you believed. The feelings generated around these situations go somewhere and are often shoved down to hopefully be forgotten. If you shove down enough emotions, over a period of time they manifest in your body, sometimes showing up as an ache or pain. For example, some experience a constriction in their breathing and chest area when confronted with overwhelming situations. As I mention throughout this book, the mind and body are connected. Medical science has been slow in looking at this, but more and more data is becoming available in this area. Dr. Candace Pert offers a plethora of information in her books about this topic.

This is all about emotional mastery. When you master the awareness of emotions, you empower yourself to choose. If you feel that there is some forgiveness to work on in your life or an issue to resolve, I encourage you to seek the support necessary to do so. Your pastor or a professional counselor can offer such support. A counselor is well worth the investment to let go of this heavy bag of emotional garbage and move forward in life!

Bible Passages: John 8:31–32
Colossians 3:12–14
Ephesians 4: 25–32

"Forgiveness: The ability to let go of our judgment and condemnation, no matter how justified that condemnation is."
— Pastor Lynn Miller

Chapter 14

🌿 PERPETUAL MOTION: STOP THE CLOCK!

The concept of time can be deadly, literally as well as metaphorically. I was once told by an insurance adjuster that he notices more car accidents when we change the clocks to daylight savings time. This makes sense. We tend to live by the clock anyway, and when we change it by an hour, it throws off the rhythm we have been in. We feel it. Many may find themselves feeling rushed because of the change. This can lead to not being present in the moment and not paying attention on the road. Can you think of how this dynamic shows up for you anywhere? Do you find yourself rushing through your life and not being present in the moment?

Some lead lifestyles of constant movement and rushing—they don't wait for daylight savings time. This is a lifestyle of adrenaline. They seem to be in anxiety mode most of the time, always rushing like a little mouse scurrying to and fro, always on the adrenaline high. These people also appear to not be listening, and they aren't, much of the time. When in conversation, they are busy thinking about what has to be done or some other scenario. You might assume people on an adrenaline high would jump from airplanes or climb cliffs. Not necessarily; there is plenty of opportunity out there to get a little juice from the adrenal glands.

The thought pattern that accompanies this is one of living in the future or the past, and rarely in the present moment. People who live a lifestyle of adrenaline think of deadlines and consequences if they don't reach the finish line. They rush around in their driving, in their movement, and even in their speech. Some even create drama in their life or gravitate to drama to keep up the rush. The fuller they can pile their plates with distractions, the better. Some are control freaks who get a rush when things are spinning out of control. I believe that an addiction to this lifestyle can develop. When I see this in my practice, and I begin to request that the individual slow down, his or her resistance usually shows up immediately. It is like asking a smoker to lay down the cigarettes and walk away. It isn't going to happen that easily. Thus, the journey begins for the individual who is embarking on the path of peace. The rushed individual does not feel peace in his or her life. The head is noisy and the body fatigued.

If this describes you, I invite you to begin the process of slowing. Your life is actually more productive when you move into balance because you are more aware of the opportunities that come your way. If you are running at breakneck speed most of the time, you are most likely running past opportunities that could lead you to where you really want to go. You are like a horse running out of control.

The big shift for someone like this comes with the realization that doing more does not result in more money, productivity, or self-value. The other problem with this lifestyle is health. With all of this rushing around, the body suffers for various reasons. One reason is that nutrition goes out the window. The market has risen to the occasion by providing fast foods that you can either go to a drive through and get or put into a microwave and "nuke." This is not truly feeding the body.

First, I don't need to give you a fast-food nutrition speech. There is plenty of literature about this subject. Second, they call microwaving "nuking" for a reason. I have heard that it kills some of the nutritional value of your food. Also, when you are shoving down your food, are you chewing it properly? God gave us teeth to chew and prepare the food for the stomach to finish digesting. Digestion begins in the mouth. Really.

So, what is the person living in the adrenaline/anxiety loop to do? Well, there are changes to be implemented. The rate of change depends on the individual. I have met certifiable adrenaline junkies, and they did not just slam on the brakes.

To begin with, look at what can be shoved off of your plate. You may be over-obligated in life. You have heard the saying, "Just say *no*." Practice this! Draw some boundaries with others. Again, a good resource for this is *Boundaries*. Drop out of the drama circle. Picture the perfect day of peace. How does that compare with how your days are going now? Make small adjustments so the two pictures begin to match. What needs to change, or better yet, disappear to move toward peace? Work out a 12-step program around this hamster-wheel lifestyle. Find a coach or counselor who has worked with this type of issue before.

You will know you are hooked in this loop when you begin justifying the triggers and behaviors that hold you in it. Or you tell yourself, "Just one more time." This is a sign for you to stop and re-evaluate, after taking a deep cleansing breath—you probably haven't done that in awhile, either!

Chapter 15

THE DELUSION OF CONTROL

Control is an elusive dynamic that is easy to get caught up in. It will exhaust even the most energetic people. We can attempt to control others, the environment, and outcomes. Some seem highly successful at control, and others find themselves disgruntled and worn out at the end of the day.

Control occurs in different scenarios. For instance, in the sales arena, it is easy to think that an outcome will be achieved each day. Perhaps the sales professional chooses a goal of a 1,000 dollars a day or 10 face-to-face selling appointments each day. It is good to have a daily goal, but focusing on the outcome can leave you frustrated, tired, and eventually burned out.

My point here is that you want to focus on what you truly have control over in the situation. The sales professional has no control over how much the customer will buy nor does he or she have control over outside circumstances that may interfere with the scheduled appointment. I do not want to take away from the art of selling. It *is* an art, and some are better at it than others, but there is a certain level of control that no one possesses, and we have to be willing to work with that. Among the things that the sales professional does have control over is how many times the phone is dialed each day and how many people are approached with the opportunity to hold a face-to-face appointment. That is within reach. Some companies have statistics that show the activity-level correlations with outcomes. That might be a good place to start in this situation.

Controlling others on a personal level is exhausting, too. Control dynamics show up in our interactions with others. When children are young, a level of control is in place to protect them, but when they are grown and out on their own, control by parents tends to distance adult children from their parents. We humans tend to exert control when we feel insecure and fearful. It can become a need to be in control. If you have ever been through a divorce, you have probably experienced the power plays of control, such as over who gets what property and custody of the pets and children.

I have also encountered managers who believe they are in control of what people do and how they react to situations. They feel in control because they think they can get people to do or not do things out of fear of losing their jobs. Managing out of fear and intimidation is not leadership, nor is it actually being in control of others. We simply do not possess the power on that level. Only God can move people.

We can also allow ourselves to be controlled by others when we alter our decisions based on what we believe others will think of us. Some hold themselves back from excelling in their careers because they fear what others will think of them if they aren't able to maintain a new level of achievement.

We move into control when we start telling God how the plan is supposed to happen. For instance, let's say that you want a sports car. You think that the only way to obtain the car is through saving money and working hard. What if you achieved it with ease? What if you got it next week through some weird twist of fate? It could happen. My point is, when you focus on only one way and believe that other avenues are not possible, you will get what you look for. Instead, you should focus on what you want and be open to receiving it. As you move closer and closer to what you want, you might be surprised at how differently it can flow to you.

In a business that relies on employees' performance, it is easy to get locked in the dynamic of holding expectations about them. When employees don't bring the desired outcome, control-mongers become disappointed, focusing on how their desired goal is not being met. Remember, where you focus is growing because you are investing energy in it. This is where surrender can help tremendously. If you find you are attached to an outcome, you are trying to control. For instance, you may have a quota to achieve by the end of the month. You have five team members in your organization who can contribute to that quota. You figure that all of them will contribute 200 dollars toward that quota, but three of them do nothing. What do you do? Get disappointed and mad? Stomp around because you are not getting what you want when you want it? No! You continue focusing on your goal (destination) and remain open to adding people who are more like you in achieving goals. As the old saying goes, "Some will, some won't, so what?"

You do not give over control of your destiny to those who are not performing. Stay the course and choose to win. Be the person you need to be to get what you want.

Chapter 16

ENERGY LOSS: DRAINS AND DISTRACTIONS

Another aspect that stops us is drains and distractions. These are the things and people that distract us and drain energy from us. Think of your mind like the hard drive of a computer; if you allow a bunch of spam and pop-ups onto your hard drive, how efficiently does the system operate? Using the computer becomes frustrating, and eventually it will run out of hard drive space to load any good, productive programs. This is what happens when we allow things to pile up in life and allow others to run their number on us. The following is a sample list of things that you might find on your energy leaks list.

>Squeaky wheel on the car
>Cluttered closet
>Annoying co-worker or boss
>Worn-out carpeting
>Stack of leads to call
>Cluttered desk
>Home repairs

You get the idea. Take an inventory of your drains and distractions. You may be amazed at how many were taking up space and energy on the hard drive of your mind. In order to erase them, you can begin with the worksheet provided **in the reference section.**

You will notice that you need to add to your list, as they will crop up periodically. Writing about them allows you to delete them from the hard drive (the mind) when they appear in your conscious thoughts. You can then begin the process of eliminating them.

"How do I do that?" you may ask. Unfortunately, it is not like a grocery list that you can take care of all at once. However, you can certainly take steps every day toward eliminating these drains and distractions.

For instance, if you want to repair or replace something that is more expensive than you can afford at the time, get a jar or establish an account to begin saving for that goal. When you drop money in, see the energy leak handled in the way that you would like. In the case of worn-out carpeting, every time you drop money in the jar, you visualize your flooring the way you wish to see it ultimately. Even a dime in the jar adds energy to what you want; this puts out the energy toward what you want. Remember, money is manifested energy.

I have my own synchronicity in this situation. Check out the dynamic and see if there is hidden money or value in your life. The carpeting in my home was worn out. My husband and I were consistent in our desire and mental creation of wanting tile in our home. It is better for my allergies and easier to clean. I had been accumulating points on a charge card that I pay off each month, but paid little attention to it. I would see my point balance accumulating over the years and kept thinking that I would one day use the points to take a cruise or other trip. After learning that I could use the points for gift cards as well as other items, I realized that I had enough points to buy gift cards at the local home store. The old carpeting went out the door, and new tile went in. I cannot express the energy I gained from handling this vampire. It is a joy to walk in my front door and see beautiful tile. Some of you may read this and think, "A monkey would have known to use the points from the charge card." However, it demonstrates that we can easily overlook hidden value in our lives, and this holds us back from having more of what we want in life.

What about the people on your energy leaks list? They require boundaries. Boundaries are loving and gentle, not hateful and hurtful. To illustrate boundaries, imagine that you are a castle. The castle has a moat around it. The castle has control over the drawbridge. You can lower the drawbridge and let people in or keep it up and keep others out of your space. Boundaries are placed to protect us and ultimately demonstrate our standards.

For example, let's say a coworker keeps dropping by your desk and chatting. This chatting distracts you from working, and you get behind in your work. Do you sit there and listen, or do you define who you are in that moment? Consider whether you enjoy the chat. If you do, explain that you really want to chat, and ask the coworker to wait until break time or lunch, because you wish to get all of your work done beforehand. If you don't like the chatting, explain that you need to stay on task, and dropping by to chat with you is not supporting you in getting your work done.

I have worked with many who have boundary issues at home. One common boundary issue I see is one spouse not being supportive of the other spouse's personal or professional goal. Sometimes, it appears that he or she is attempting to sabotage the goal. We can't change others, but we can set boundaries to be respected. We can simply state, "That doesn't work for me," or "This doesn't feel loving and supportive of my goal." You have to be willing to draw the line in the sand without being accusatory. Telling someone that he or she is sabotaging you probably won't be heard or well received. If you state how you feel and own those feelings, it may get you farther along the path. Learning to draw boundaries takes practice if you are not already adept at it. You may also find that it is easier to draw boundaries with some people than it is with others.

If someone is a drain on you, he or she needs to be on the energy leaks list. You can begin the steps of drawing boundaries with that person. He or she may test your boundaries for awhile, but eventually will give up and stop the behavior or stay out of your space. Either way, you win.

There is great material out there on the subject. If you find yourself struggling in the area of boundaries, I recommend reading *Boundaries,* mentioned earlier.

The bottom line is that you have to keep your mental hard drive clean and operating optimally. The more space you create in your life by eliminating what you don't want, the more room you have for good things to flow in.

Proverbs 13:20

Chapter 17

THE UNDERTOW OF THOUGHT AND EMOTION

There is a stream of thought running in our minds at all times. It can be a positive and uplifting stream, or it can be much like the undertow in the ocean, which can pull you a long way if you get caught up in it. I have heard that the best thing to do if caught in the undertow is to ride it out until it stops pulling on you, and then swim back in or swim sideways out of it. We can do the same thing when we get caught in the negative mental undertow, but we first have to realize that we are caught up in it.

The undertow shows up when we embark on a journey toward something new and wonderful. It can be like a little negative voice in the back of your mind. For example, you are at the grocery store and wish to hand your business card to someone who seems like a good prospect. You reach for your card, and the little voice says, "Go ahead, and if you do, you will hear the loudspeaker announcing you on aisle three!" You put the card back in your pocket and continue to allow negative programming (which is a lie) to hold you back. Notice the emotion that can be attached to this thinking.

You can say affirmations or flood yourself with positive messaging and still find yourself caught in the undertow of a story that holds you back. It is tricky because it feels and sounds real. You begin to believe your own press release. The best example I can think of to illustrate just how powerful your thoughts can be is the movie *The Matrix*. When Neo is being shot at and realizes the bullets aren't real, he redefines them. Those bullets represent your undertow. You can allow them to penetrate you and take you down or you can say no to them and stop them from stopping you. Choose to win!

The undertow is a combination of thoughts and emotion. The emotion adds a charge to the thoughts. You may have thoughts of abundance, but if the undertow is charged with strong emotions of scarcity and fear, it negates the thoughts of abundance. For example, if an individual states that he wants financial freedom and abundance, he builds an affirmation around it and says it regularly. But when he spends a majority of his time in the undertow of worry about money and focused on fear of not having enough, guess what shows up? Scarcity. This is because his dominant thought is focused on fear and scarcity. How you think affects how you feel. How you feel affects behavior, body language, facial expression, how you speak, and the energy dynamics in and around you in God Space.

An individual may say that he uses affirmations and stays positive throughout the day, but the undertow can be like a stream in the background. It is playing much of the time on low volume while he is distracted by things that tell him that what he doesn't want is real. Let's take this a step further:

THOUGHTS
⬇
FEELINGS
⬇
BEHAVIOR
BODY LANGUAGE
FACIAL EXPRESSION
SPEECH
ENERGY
⬇
RESULTS/YOUR OUTWARD WORLD

Chapter 18

🌿 THE THREE Rs

Here is what to do when you are caught in the undertow. I offer you the Three Rs. It used to be reading, writing, and 'rithmetic. It is now Recognize, Release, and Replace.

Recognize that you are caught in the undertow when you feel an energy drop. You may also feel fearful or you may just notice that you are slowing down in pursuing your goal, if you are not already stopped. Creative avoidance and distractions are clues that you are caught in the undertow.

Release the energy that is holding you back. There are thought patterns associated with emotions that are holding you back, and these need to be released to facilitate forward movement toward your goal.

In order to release these patterns, find a quiet place without distractions. Sit down and relax. Take about four deep breaths while counting to four with each breath. Just focus on your breathing while you connect with yourself. Imagine that you are blowing all of the thoughts and feelings into a balloon. See yourself tying off the balloon. Then release it to float up to God. Imagine the hand of God reaching down for the balloon and transforming it. Maybe God takes the balloon away or pops it. Whatever works for you—it's your visual.

Notice how you are feeling as you do the exercise. My clients have offered variations on this; use what works for you. You might also just imagine yourself exhaling the nonsupportive thoughts and feelings with each breath until they are gone.

Replace your undertow with positive, loving, and uplifting material. This is where an affirmation can come in handy. I like to begin affirmations with "I am..." because this keeps it in the present moment. You want to state the affirmation and really experience it. Since you are already sitting in a quiet place, visualize yourself where you want to be or see yourself experiencing something that really excites you. You are raising the energy level within yourself. Charge it with the emotions that come with the replacement thought. You want to really live there in that moment.

Bible Passage:
Romans 12:2. This passage confirms the need to renew the mind and live in God's reality. We live in God's reality, and in that reality anything is possible!

Chapter 19

🖋 THE BOX OF NEGATIVE MENTAL UNDERTOW

To further illustrate how the undertow stops us, look at the following page. Write your name at the top and whatever goal you desire at the bottom. Inside the box, write all of the undertow you think and feel about yourself and moving toward that goal. For instance, your undertow box might have statements like this:

> It's too hard.
> I'm not educated enough.
> They will tell me no.
> I'm confused.
> It's a bad time to call.
> I have other things like dishes that need to be done instead.
> I'm not attractive or talented enough.
> I'm too tired.
> I'm a lousy money manager.
> I don't know how to…

You get the idea. Write down any thought that does not support forward movement toward your goal.

Your name _____

Your Goal _____

Once you have placed your undertow thoughts in the box, take a look at all the lies you tell yourself to either slow yourself down or stop on the path to your success. Considering that the shortest distance between two points is a straight line, draw a line from your name (this represents you) to your goal. Do you see where you get off the path to success? It is nothing more than thoughts and feelings.

Once the undertow has been identified, now what? You can decide what you want to do with it now. Do you want to believe it and stop, or do you want to acknowledge that it is there and keep on going? It is your choice. Again, we have a constant stream of thought and we think and feel many things. It is our choice whether we believe it and act on it. You can use the three Rs with this. The box is recognizing what you are telling yourself. Now release it. You can imagine the hand of God touching it and transforming it, and then write in the supportive statements to move you forward. Do whatever works for you. In the workshops I lead, we deal with the stuff in this box to release you and move forward.

Chapter 20

THE FORMULA TO NEUTRALIZE PROCRASTINATION

Another tool to handle the undertow when it stops you is with the procrastination formula. When we mentally move into fear, we go into fight, flight, or freeze. Here is the tool to use when you freeze up. Once you become aware that you are frozen in procrastination,

1. Stop and breathe!

2. Finish this sentence: "I don't want to do this because…" Let your undertow talk here. Listen to what it is saying.

3. What am I telling myself to continue procrastinating? This is the point at which you look at the underlying message (or lie) that you are telling yourself.

4. What evidence do I have that any of this is true? If you were presenting evidence in court to support the undertow thinking, what would it be?

You are not finished applying the formula yet. I want to point out that so far you have identified your faulty thinking and debunked it.

5. What am I risking by standing frozen in procrastination? Examine the goals and dreams from which you are holding yourself back by not taking action in this very moment.

6. What am I risking by taking a step toward my success? Examine the actual risk involved if you just take that step right now.

7. What am I willing to do right now? This is the only question you need to remember in this formula. It is the action step. What counts is what you are willing to do in each moment. It is about being willing rather than being disciplined. You have to be willing to do something; forcing yourself through it doesn't sound joyful to me. Be willing to be uncomfortable and do it anyway. Willingness is surrender.

Right now is the only moment that you ever have to change your future. Where you are in your life or career right now is the result of the decisions you have made on a moment-to-moment basis. If you don't like where you are right now, all you have to do is begin making different decisions. I'm not talking about big decisions. It might be as simple as making a phone call or having a conversation that you have been putting off.

Fear is about the past or the future. It rarely has much to do with the present moment unless you are standing on a snake. Take the opportunity to get present in the moment, put on your blinders, and run for the finish line. Just because you think it and feel it does not make it true. As the cartoon character Maxine says, "Don't believe everything you think!"

If you are procrastinating, you may notice that much of your action is based on faulty undertow thinking. It is time to take your power back and act from truth. This formula is designed to help you arrive at your truth in moment-to-moment decisions and actions, which leads to living in truth more and more in your life. When you choose to live in that truth, you empower yourself to greatness.

An Example of the Procrastination Formula:

Let's just say that it is time for you to exercise, but you are procrastinating.

1. *Stop and breathe!* What are you feeling and thinking? You might be thinking, "Man, that is boring. I can do it tomorrow. I am too tired, and exercise is painful."

2. *I don't want to do this because* I am too tired. I hate to exercise.

3. *What am I telling myself to continue to procrastinate?* Basically, the self-messaging is pointing out that there is no benefit to exercising

The Formula to Neutralize Procrastination

and it is unimportant. The fact that exercise gives you energy is being overlooked.

4. *What evidence do I have that any of this is true?* Let's look at the above mental undertow. Exercise gives you energy, so you will feel better afterward. You hold a more positive view of yourself when you practice good self-care, so you can gain a sense of well being from exercise. There is no evidence supporting the mind chatter in steps 1 and 2.

5. *What am I risking by staying frozen in procrastination?* It really depends on your situation. Perhaps the extra weight is posing some health problems. Maybe you want to get back into the clothes you wore last year or you are headed to your 20-year class reunion and want to look buff! Whatever the case, there is a risk involved.

6. *What am I risking by taking a step toward success?* You are risking feeling sweaty and rejuvenated. You are risking having more dirty laundry as a result of the sweaty gym clothes.

7. *What am I willing to do right now?* Whatever you decide here. Hopefully, you will take a step in the direction of the changes that you want. It is the decisions that you make on a moment-to-moment basis that land you where you are. Where you are right now is the result of the decisions you have made on a moment-to-moment basis.

Let's use the formula to examine a situation that applies to many business people. Perhaps a list of prospects needs to be called today, and procrastination sets in.

1. *Stop and breathe!* Get present with yourself.

2. *I don't want to do this because* the prospects will tell me no. No one will be interested. I have nothing to offer. The people I call are monitoring their caller ID. It is their break time or dinner time, and I will be bothering them. They are at lunch. The list goes on and on.

3. *What am I telling myself to continue procrastinating?* There is a devaluing of the product or service being offered. There is also an attitude that the calls will be fruitless.

4. *What evidence do I have that any of this is true?* Basically, the message in the above undertow is that it is a waste of time. One of the most common things I hear in this scenario is that everyone told the caller no on a previous day. Or perhaps no one answered the last 10 calls dialed. Be aware that the present moment has nothing to do with the past. Just because 10 people told you no does not mean that the next person is going to do so.

5. *What am I risking by staying frozen in procrastination?* Income is usually impacted by new business. Your position or job may be in jeopardy if quotas are not met. You may also be risking your goals and dreams. That is important.

6. *What am I risking by taking a step toward my success?* You might hear the word no. You might hear the word yes. You might get an answering machine. Any way it goes, you are closer to the desired destination. You must go through the no to get to the yes.

7. *What am I willing to do right now?* Perhaps make five calls, and then take a break. Some people find that they make the five calls and keep going, because they find it easier than before they started. If you make different decisions, you'll get different results

Creative avoidance is another form of procrastination. This occurs when you convince yourself that menial tasks are more important than what you know needs to be done to support success. How often have you caught yourself doing dishes or running errands instead of sticking to business? Maybe a birthday party becomes the reason that you go off of your diet. What do you choose? Choices made on a moment-to-moment basis will determine the future! What do you choose?

Chapter 21

🌿 THE DEPTH OF LOVE AND YOUR DESERVE LEVEL

I often hear the question "How do I raise my deserve level?" Wow, that is a loaded question that can mean a lifetime of work; that's not a bad thing, however.

> Why do you deserve whatever you are wanting?
>
> What undertow do you hear or feel as you state what you want and why you deserve it?
>
> What false (and probably old) beliefs do you hold in the undertow?

I spent a great deal of time being stumped in this area as I began exploring the dynamic of deserving. The synchronicities began to appear for me around the Bible passage, John 3:16. I was asking God for clarity on the subject, and for quite awhile I noticed John 3:16 in the oddest places, even though it was not yet the Christmas season. When I encountered it, I read John 3:16 over and over. I began getting frustrated and said, "Okay, I get it. You gave your only son because you loved us." Then, there it was again. This cycle went on for months, and I began to doubt myself. Would I ever get what God was trying to tell me?

Then it all began to unravel. I was in Oklahoma, on my way home from Houston, Texas, and decided to pull into a truck stop to gas up and use the restroom. I came out of the restroom and, not paying attention, bumped into a display rack. I spun around and the first thing on that display rack that I saw was a brilliant green t-shirt with the cutest pink bunny extending his arms out. The saying below the bunny was, *YOU ARE LOVED! John 3:16.*

I was stunned. I stood there and wondered if I should buy the shirt. I also felt frustration at a new level because I felt as if I still wasn't getting what God was telling me. I left that truck stop wondering, *"What—What—What is it?! I don't get what you are trying to tell me Lord!"* No, I didn't buy the shirt.

I drove on home, wondering if I would ever get the message. I felt the journey continue. The next week, I was talking to an acquaintance about the law of attraction. I asked, "What do you think are the big pieces that we miss about the law of attraction?" He replied, "You know, the biggest piece is love." It began to sink in, but there was still no eureka moment. You could almost see the little puff of smoke above my head as I drove home that evening.

Two days later, at church, the holy two-by-four struck me between the eyes. The Pastor said something that made me nearly fall out of my chair. During the sermon he asked a very pointed question. "Would you allow your child to be sacrificed in the manner that Jesus was to save the world if you had the power to stop it?" First, I had a human reaction. I thought, "Well, hell no, you can take me, but not my son!"

Then the holy two-by-four hit me: the depth of God's love is unfathomable to us. I was shaken in that moment. I suddenly knew that I'd received the message. I drove home from church and sat in front of the fire, pondering what had happened. I had felt it in my very being, deep in my soul. That was it. I stared out the window and asked God to show me that level of love. He answered with a moment of experience. It was a moment of peace, expansion, and knowing that he is here all the time—here in the sense of being everything, not simply an external entity. I didn't want to leave the feeling when I was coming out of it. It was a moment without time.

Look at the deserve level here. We humans were certainly a mess at the time that Christ walked the earth. We continue to be a mess, but we have been forgiven because we are loved. We are loved in spite of our humanness and tendencies to falter, yet we beat ourselves up over petty things.

Why do we find it difficult to love ourselves in a way that is not narcissistic? How much do you love yourself? How do you treat yourself? To love your self is to love God. He is the creator. He loves us very much, and we treat ourselves like donkey droppings at times, especially when it comes to winning big in life. We can hold ourselves back from greatness. Self-abandonment occurs at times when we disrepect ourselves and stop on the path to success. It's as if we encounter an obstacle that triggers fear and we jump ship, but God is still there! This undermines faith.

The Depth of Love and Your Deserve Level

In order to live in God Space and attract who and what you want, you have to walk in faith, knowing that whatever you are moving toward is coming even when it doesn't seem like it.

Your faith determines the energy frequency running in your mind and, ultimately, in your body. Hope is right in there with faith. You have the option to focus on (invest in) whatever you wish. Remembering that we live in God's reality, and in that reality anything is possible, why would you choose to live in less than joy and love?

What tells you that you do or don't deserve whatever you want in life?

What is right and beautiful about you?

1.

2.

3.

How can you show yourself and God some love today?

1.

2.

3.

Bible passage: John 3:16

Chapter 22

🌿 THE LOOP OF GRATITUDE AND FAITH

Even the best-laid plans can fall apart in the midst of action. We begin forward movement, and the results that we expect do not occur. What then? We have a choice. We can become disappointed and focus on all the negativity in the situation. Sometimes, we have a little temper tantrum and throw in the towel. In other words, we become very focused on what we don't want, we begin investing in just that, and we abandon the path—or we can re-focus on the destination and keep on marching.

Worry can set in and undermine faith. Worrying is the act of focusing on what you don't want. It ultimately causes hesitation, if not disaster, on the path to success. It is wasted energy and time, because you are standing still, fearing (note that there is usually emotion charging this scenario) that what you don't want to happen will happen.

Remember, as you walk the path of success, you will not always have the answers. You have to be willing to walk in faith. God respects faith and responds to it. If you are attached to the outcome in a situation, you, in essence, are telling God how to do His job, which is not a good plan. God knows what you want and will deliver in a bigger fashion than you can imagine.

Your best strategy when your plans fall apart is to allow yourself to express and release your disappointment, then collect yourself to get back in the saddle and move on down the path. Move in faith that your destination is right around the corner.

Here is an example from my own life. I was asked to speak to an organization, and I failed to ask them what they wanted to hear about. I *assumed* that I knew a good subject to give a talk on. I launched into my chosen subject, which flopped. I changed gears and began to talk about a different subject, and it too wasn't well received. I finally stopped and asked the assembled group what they wanted me to discuss, and it wasn't a topic that I could have imagined. I attempted to move forward from there, but the moment was lost, and it wasn't one of my more notable evenings. The moral of the above story is, get directions before embarking on any journey or when you are lost.

After that experience, I could have decided that I was no good at public speaking and given up. I embraced it as a learning experience and moved on, focusing on what I would do differently the next time.

In following God's lead, we will encounter difficulties. Think of the difficulties (that is putting it lightly) that Jesus encountered. Remember, there is no failure, there are only opportunities to learn more about your pursuits and about yourself. Be willing to take risks along the path. I have heard numerous successful people state that they encountered problems more than once along the path to success. Instead of giving up on their goals and dreams, they chose to keep on going. This is an area where faith and focus can be strengthened.

Where have you allowed disappointment and worry to stop you or alter your direction? What are you allowing to control your time, emotions, goals, and energy right now?

When you encounter disappointment, this is a perfect opportunity to reconnect with God. If something isn't working out, it doesn't mean that you will never get to where you want to go. A song by Garth Brooks, *Unanswered Prayers,* comes to mind. I can relate to that song, because I run into past flames here and there. Of course, they probably feel the same way. There is always the next opportunity out there. It is usually bigger and better than what did not turn out for you this time. Not just in relationships, but in everything you set out to reach for.

Faith is knowing or expecting that what you are seeking is there. When you feel disappointed, instead of allowing it to undermine your faith, take some time to talk with God about the wonderful things happening in your life. Be grateful for the things you want that are not yet in front of you. Thank God, not with mindless words, but with feeling. This brings us closer to Him through the dialogue.

One quick trick to this is to make what I call a blessings charge card. This is a charge card that has zero interest rate, no annual fee, and no spending limit.! It's simple to make. Just cut out a credit card–sized piece of card stock. Write at least 10 things that are going well in your life right now. For example, good health, employed, healthy children, pets you love, good marriage, etc. You can write on the front and back, and laminate it, too. (You can find laminating pouches at office supply stores.) Keep it in your wallet. When you find that your focus has shifted and your faith is waning, whip out the card and charge yourself up. You want to focus on the strengths in your life and expand them. Come from a place of strength and gratitude; this builds faith. There is no sense investing energy in what you don't want. The return is negative.

What and where you focus on will expand. If you dwell in scarcity and fear, this is the state of mind, body, and, ultimately, being that you will create. Your body and energy follow what you focus upon.

Bible Passages:
Matthew 6:25–34. This passage reminds us to release worry. Worrying is focused on the future. We need to be looking at what is before us today, right now, in the present moment. Walk in faith—God provides.

Hebrews 11:1

Matthew 9:28–30

Chapter 23

🌿 FOCUS: AN INVESTMENT OF ENERGY

Pretend you have just won 10 million dollars in a lottery. Do you invest it, or do you run to the casino and gamble it all? Either decision will yield a return. Invested wisely, your money will yield a positive return. If frittered away, it will yield a negative return.

How you choose to focus determines the return on your energy. The act of focusing is investing your energy. If you focus on what you want, you get closer to it through your actions and by looking for signs that you are getting closer to your goal. If you focus on what you don't want, you get closer to that through the actions you take or don't take, and you tend to look for evidence that what you don't want is happening. You may ask, "Why would anyone do that?" We all do it at one time or another. For example, you might get a scratchy throat and begin to worry about getting a cold. You can even verbalize it: "I hope I am not getting a cold!" You have just verbally affirmed an illness by sending energy into what you don't want. The converse to this scenario would be, "I am healthy and balanced!" You could use any affirmation of health in this scenario.

Try this exercise:

>   Look around you right now for everything you see that is brown.

>   Look around and notice everything round.

>   Look around and notice everything blue.

Think for a moment about how many things you noticed that were square.

You see what you look for. If what you are seeing is not what you want, look for the things and events that are what you want. A quick way to feel better is to forgo the evening news for a few days. What are you accomplishing by bombarding yourself with the hate and disaster in the world one or two times per day? The shortest distance between two points is a direct line. Why would you waste time running off the path to success by choosing to run through the underbrush and briars of scarcity and fear when there is a clear-cut path?

"I am" statements are another way to invest energy into what you want. Commonly called affirmations, these state what you want or who you choose to be in that moment. If you develop an affirmation with futuristic language, you keep it off in your future. For example:

"I am a millionaire!" vs. "I will be a millionaire!"

"I am looking fit and fine in my new suit." vs. "I will be looking fit and fine in my new suit."

You get the idea. You want to address and affirm what you want as if it is already true. Remember, the more you live there mentally, the closer it gets!

What do you do if you create "I am" statements and the undertow creeps in? Let's say that you affirm that you are a millionaire and then your undertow says, "Yeah, right! You don't have a dime in the bank—you know you're broke!" Remember the three Rs? Here is an opportunity to practice them. You can also develop some "allowing" statements, giving yourself permission to win:

"I allow myself millionaire status!"

"I allow one million dollars to accumulate in my bank account!"

Sometimes, it takes only a small shift in what we are verbalizing to get the energy flowing in the appropriate direction. What is the root of what is holding you back? Are you focused on finding solutions and healing? Create some "I am" statements to support forward movement in this area.

Bible Passage: Acts 3:1–8 is an example of the power of focus. Note that the beggar is focused on receiving money instead of focusing on the root of his problem. Peter tells him to focus on healing the problem (being crippled), and the beggar is healed.

Part 2

Accelerate on the Path to Success!

Chapter 24

🌿 BEGIN EACH DAY WITH NOURISHMENT

Once you move around the obstacles and find yourself cruising on the path to success, there are some things you can do to accelerate toward your destination. Because you will find what you look for, it is important to invest your energy and receive what you want with clear intention.

The following are exercises and ideas for you to begin applying on a daily basis to bring you closer to your destination. These are not exercises to do once or just a few times. They need to become a regular part of who you are. In doing so, you support your shift in focus onto what you want. You become more intentional in your day-to-day movement toward the destination.

It is common to either not do them or do them for awhile and then stop. Decide that you are focused on winning and be willing to do whatever it takes to reach your destination! Be willing to *be* different so that you *do* different and *have* different. What does your undertow have to say about this?

Begin Each Day with Nourishment

We have all heard that we should start our day with a balanced breakfast. This feeds the body. What about the mind and spirit? The tone of each day is set in the morning. If you wake up and begin your day with dread, what is the rest of your day usually like? Why not begin each day with a balanced breakfast for body, mind, and spirit?

You can figure out the balanced food part. What does a nourishing and balanced breakfast for mind and spirit look like to you? Perhaps it is quiet time to listen to God. Maybe an inspirational CD, passage from the Bible, or section from a book will feed your mind and spirit.

Do you feel that you just can't do that because there isn't enough time or your job and marriage are just miserable? Remember, you are the driver of your mind—it does not drive you. You choose how you start each day. Happiness is an inside job. Set the tone. What do you choose today?

Suggested nourishing meals for mind and spirit:

Claim Your Victory Today by Dr. Creflo A. Dollar

Daily Readings from Your Best Life Now: 90 Devotions for Living at Your Full Potential by Joel Osteen

Jesus, CEO by Laurie Beth Jones

Life in the Word Devotional by Joyce Meyer

Chapter 25

SUPERCHARGE YOUR ENERGY INVESTMENT

This exercise involves finding a power partner. Make sure that your power partner, like you, wants more on the bottom line of life. You do not want to team up with someone who is negative. Find someone who is willing to talk with you, either by phone or in person, at least once a week. It is good to hold each other accountable about your activity grids (in the reference section or at www.loranewman.com) and do the following exercise.

I call this exercise the "as if" exercise. A psychologist named Alfred Adler developed the theoretical base for this exercise. Basically, you will call your power partner or meet with him or her in person and pretend that you have already arrived at your goal (destination). You tell the person all about the event. Move into the emotions that you will feel upon arriving at the goal (destination).

For example, let's say that your 90-day destination is to sell 100 widgets or to lose 20 pounds. When it is time to call or meet your power partner, simply take a moment to envision yourself actually depositing the money from the hundredth sale of widgets or getting into the outfit you will wear when you are at your desired weight. See yourself there, feel the moment, and hear the sounds that accompany the experience. Call your power partner and begin the conversation as you would *as if* it were already true and a real experience.

Your power partner's role is to give feedback to you *as if* your destination has been achieved. The partner plays along and asks the questions that come to mind in that situation. Remember to keep the comments and questions in the present tense because you are painting the picture *as if* it has already happened. When you feel complete with the process, switch roles and allow your power partner to take his or her turn.

Doing this exercise gives energy to your destination. Remember, the more you mentally live in your destination, the closer it gets. You supercharge the path to your destination. I used this technique much of the time when my husband and I were looking for our first home. The synchronicities fell right into place and we found the perfect home—or, should I say, it found us?

Here is how it happened. After months of disagreement about which home we should buy, I had reached an uncomfortable level of frustration and was growing exhausted. We seemed to always disagree about the size of the home or the location.

I began doing the "as if" exercise, first with my husband. This made sense, right? We both wanted a home, so it was logical to me that we should do the exercise together. *Wrong!*

I did not take into account my husband's "Show me" personality. He is detail oriented, quite logical, and step wise in his thinking. His is a nice balance to my personality, which is not so logical, step wise, and detail oriented. He basically told me that the exercise was nice, but the house I was describing in the exercise was off in our distant future. That angered me, and I became more determined to find our home. I did the exercise with other people who were willing to play with me. That was in January of that year. We moved into the house that I was describing in June of the same year. As a bonus, God threw in a hot tub. What a great God we have.

It was synchronistic how I found the house, as it was not even officially on the market yet. I was scanning the newspaper one Sunday and found a listing for a horse ranch. No price was listed. Out of curiosity, I called the realtor listing it. She gave me the property's specifics. The barn sounded nicer than the house. It was out of our price range, and I thanked her for the information. I was prepared to hang up when she said, "Tell me what you are looking for." I wanted a home with land and amenities for horses.

She explained that a home owner had just signed a contract with her that day to sell his house, which had everything that I had just described to her. I agreed to drive out and take a look at it. I didn't know what I would do if I liked it, because my husband was out of town for two weeks.

Sure enough, after taking a tour, I knew in my spirit that I had found our home. I called my husband and sent him pictures by e-mail. We got all of the paperwork in order, and bought the home before he even got to walk on the property. Talk about a leap of faith on his part. His friends told him that he either trusted me unequivocally or he was crazy.

I drove him out to see the property on Easter Sunday. He walked through the house and took me to the deck off the back door and hugged me. He had tears in his eyes as he said, "You did good, dear." I can't convey how much that meant to me.

I found the home that we both wanted; it was bigger and better than we imagined we would find. The bonus I mentioned earlier occurred because the owners decided to leave the almost-new hot tub instead of relocating it.

Like I said, God knows what you want more than you do. Just keep putting the energy out there and walking in faith that it will happen. When you walk with the blinders on toward your destination of success and give up control, God connects you with others and the magic happens in God Space.

Chapter 26

🌿 BE THE BLESSING THAT YOU SEEK

If you want something in your life, be that blessing to others. If you want more money or freedom, how can you help others get more money or freedom?

You want to *be* whatever you want in your life. Many years ago, in coaching school, I learned the *Be-Do-Have* statement: "*Be* who you need to be, so that you can *do* what you need to do, so that you can *have* what you want to have."

This statement means that you have to be in alignment with what you want. For instance, some lottery winners are ill equipped in the money management area and eventually end up broke. They are not "being" people of integrity with their money, hence they end up right back where they started.

On the other hand, many millionaires went bankrupt at one time. They lost everything and built it back again. It comes down to who you are being on a moment-to-moment basis and where you focus. If you are being the person who just gets by, that is probably what you will do—just get by. What blessings do you seek?

Chapter 27

🌿 RECEIVE

Are you good at receiving? Do you really take the time to appreciate you and thank God for the wonderful body and mind you have? For the life you have? Receive the blessings in your life. You may be overlooking them. Think about your responses to gifts and compliments you receive. Do you think that the person giving the compliment is just being kind? Do you downplay whatever was complimented? Do you say things like, "You shouldn't have" when you receive a gift?

Stop that! Receive the compliment or gift and run like the wind. To do otherwise is to resist the blessings and love. How can you expect the blessings to find their way into your life when you refuse to receive them? That is like telling Ed McMahon to go to the neighbor's house when he is standing on your doorstep with the big check from Publisher's Clearinghouse!

If you consistently push away the good things in your life, even something as small as a compliment, how do you expect the bigger things to get into your life? You won't see it. Take time each day to be thankful for what you have. The blessings charge card I mentioned previously is a great place to start. Miracles and blessings are happening all around us. Take a good look and keep on looking for more of them: they do happen. You deserve good things. Be willing to receive them. If you struggle with this, what tells you that you don't deserve to receive great things? Refer back to the section titled "The Depth of Love and Your Deserve Level"

Chapter 28

⚑ BE WILLING

Are you willing to live in health, wellness, and abundance? If so, look within. It all starts there. Take the time to reflect and make adjustments in thinking and behavioral patterns that support the life that you desire, no matter how uncomfortable it is. Throw out the discipline dogma and *be* willing to be who you need to be so that you can *do* what you need to do to *have* what you wish to have. If you think you don't have time to live life on your terms, ask yourself what you are getting from the way things are going now. What is all the "busyness" about?

It is the daily steps and changes that add up. Even baby steps count. Be consistent in shifting your focus onto what you want. This requires you to be present in the moment, not on a mental coffee break. When you are present with your thoughts and feelings, you give yourself the power to choose. You choose what to focus on and what to think about, which ultimately affects your emotions and behavior. When you recite your affirmations, move to that place, feel it, see it, believe it. Charge them with emotional energy. This adds power and energy to whatever you are moving toward. The more you live there mentally, the closer the goal gets. Set aside time to make a winning strategy and be willing to follow it. If you need support, *get it*. If what your doctor has been prescribing is not working, it is time to do some research and look for an alternative. If your marriage or business is not working, it is time to find out how it can work. Take responsibility and make changes. It is the daily practice of being healthy, well, and abundant that leads you to where you want to go. That means *every day*. You are the driver of your mind—it does not drive you.

Bible Passage: Proverbs 23:12

Chapter 29

🌿 THROW OUT YOUR GOALS AND SET YOUR DESTINATION

Set the destination. I like the word destination. It sounds solid. The word goal is so overused that it seems people almost become desensitized to it. As a coach and counselor, I often hear, "My new goal is…," "I missed my goal," "I have set a new goal," "I fell short of my goal," etc.

Let's establish a destination. After all, an airline pilot doesn't take off down the runway with a goal—he or she has a destination. Can you imagine hearing, "Please fasten your seatbelts. Our goal today is to land in Chicago." No, thank you! What if the pilot fell short of the goal? There is intention in his or her actions. Of course the pilot is trained to handle emergencies, but rarely does he or she have to use those skills. The pilot doesn't get the plane in the air and then hesitate, only to land short of the destination. Are you prepared to set your destinations now? What is the first destination?

Chapter 30

🌱 MAKE IT REAL: VISUALIZE!

Begin setting the stage for each day. When you wake up *every day*, take a few minutes to picture yourself at your destination. Feel it. Smell it. Hear it. See it. Be it. Really get into the picture and make it your reality during this moment. The more you mentally live in the destination, the closer it gets. Supercharge your path to success! Here is how:

Set your joy scale to 10.

The joy scale is rated from 0 to 10.
0 = Yuck!
10 = Happy, Happy, Happy! Heaven on Earth!

Any time you feel less than joyful or just want to jump-start your day, close your eyes, take a deep breath and relax. Visualize yourself at your destination. What do you see, feel, smell, hear, etc.? Be in the moment of your destination until your joy scale hits 10.

Does your undertow attempt to pull you away from what you want? Notice if you found it difficult to get to 10 on the joy scale. If so, relax. Not everyone masters this right away. Keep practicing. It is like going to the gym; you have to be consistent to build the muscle.

Chapter 31

CONSISTENCY AND COMMITMENT

Consistency and commitment are the areas where many tend to go to sleep, fall back into old habits, and wander off into the woods to be forever lost. I am challenging you to stay awake and on your path to success! The very things that I mentioned in the previous pages are what happen to get us off the path. The undertow creeps in, we have an emotionally imbalanced moment, or some other event distracts us from our truth and integrity.

I often hear, "I need more discipline!" Let go of the discipline dogma and just be willing. Be willing to get back on course. Pick up where you left off, and keep putting one foot in front of the other. Being willing is an easier transition than simply being shoved into the change.

If you find yourself talking a big game and not taking any action, *phone or get out of the booth!* Be willing to take action, in spite of discomfort. It is in the consistent moment-to-moment steps that results begin to show up.

Be a blessing to someone else consistently if you are looking for blessings and miracles yourself. Be generous to experience generosity. Be grateful to experience gratefulness. Do you notice the common word in these statements? *Be*. Who you are being determines who and what shows up in your life. This is the magic of God Space. Take a look in the mirror: do you like the person you are being? If not, what adjustments need to be made?

Commitment is dedication. Commitment is doing it even when you don't want to. We honor some commitments, like marriage, but somehow we don't honor commitments to ourselves. I challenge you to recommit to you and your destination on a daily basis. Create some "I am" statements to affirm your commitment.

Your actions have to match the thoughts. If you are busy giving lip service and not backing it up with action, what results can you expect? Align your actions with your thoughts and words. This builds confidence, because you begin to trust yourself again and stop abandoning yourself in the face of adversity.

It's time to take flight in life!
Success Work Journal

When you are ready to begin your 90-day process, log onto *www.loranewman.com* and enter your information in the area called *Let the journey begin!*. These e-mails are to support your process of moving toward your destination. You will receive an e-mail each day for 90 days. Your information stays in our database and is not shared.

WISHING YOU MANY BLESSINGS
AND
MUCH ABUNDANCE
ON YOUR 90-DAY JOURNEY!

"Do or do not. There is no try."
—YODA, IN *STAR WARS*

Part 3

90-Day Success Work Journal

Planning the Journey: An Overview

Take time to really think about your answers to the questions listed on the next pages of this journal. You want to be clear and intentional in your steps down the path of success. If you are unwilling to stop long enough to take a look at where you want to go and where you want to be, then that may be an indication of why you aren't there yet. This is equivalent to jumping in the car in Missouri to head to Disney World without a map and assuming you can just drive southeast to get there.

Is not taking the time to be authentic in moving toward your destination a pattern for you? Do you think you don't have time to sit down and answer the questions? If that is the case, you may find that you don't have the time to move toward your destination.

Some people will put the journal down before completing Day 90. Remember the section about commitment on the previous page. Look at what you want, and become aware every day of where you are and what you are choosing to think and do.

As your awareness level increases, you will make changes. When you integrate those changes into your being, you may find yourself frustrated again. This is great, because it means that you are looking at raising your awareness to the next level. Embrace confusion, frustration, and paradox. They guard the gates of truth!

Enjoy the journey!

Day 1

Let's start with a clear picture. It is difficult to run after something that you can't see. In other words, if you aren't clear about the destination, how can you possibly plot a path to it?

Answer these questions on the following pages:

1. What does it mean to step into your power and live life on your terms?

2. What does it mean to you to live in God Space? (This is a place where you reach destinations and experience synchronicity, attracting who and what you want with ease, grace, and joy.)

3. Who seems to be showing up in your space right now?

4. Who do you like to spend time with?

5. Who or what do you want to stop attracting into your life?

6. Who or what do you want to start attracting into your life?

7. What is your destination right now?

8. What does your destination mean to you?

9. What will it bring to your life and the lives of others?

10. What problem(s) will it solve, if any?

11. How will you feel upon arriving at the destination? Observe the emotions that come up around your destination.

Journal your responses on the following pages.

Notes

1. Life on your terms

2. God Space

3. Who and what is showing up now

___

___

___

4. I like to spend time with

___

___

___

___

5. Stop attracting

___

___

___

___

6. Start attracting

___

___

___

___

When you examine who is showing up in your life, look at acquaintances, co-workers, clients, and relationships. When you are with these people, take note of whether you feel happy and uplifted, tired and depressed, angry, or anything at all.

Are the people around you big thinkers or do they live in fear, struggle, and scarcity? Is there much drama in their lives? Examine who you are choosing to listen to.

If you are in partnership or considering a partnership, explore the dynamics of co-creating with the other person. If the two of you are investing energy in different directions, and if your pictures don't match, this fragments the energy. Do you feel attracted to the individual or seduced and overpowered by him or her? There is a difference.

7. My destination

On Day 90 I am:

_____

What do you want? What do you really want in the next 90 days?

_____

What is your destination?

_____

Is it "doable" in 90 days? Stretch it, yet keep it real. List it all.

_____

State your destination:

_____

8. What the destination means to you

9. What it will bring to others

10. What problems it will solve

11. How you will feel upon arrival

Day 2

Get out your activity grid! After deciding on your 90-day destination, now it is time to figure out what you need to do on a daily basis to support the destination. Here is how to begin that process:

What needs to happen on a monthly basis to support the destination?

_____

_____

_____

What needs to happen on a weekly basis to support the destination?

_____

_____

_____

What needs to happen on a daily basis to support the destination?

_____

_____

_____

This is where the activity grid comes in. You can download these for free at *www.loranewman.com*. Once you have the grid in front of you, follow the directions to fill in the blanks. The idea is to create a daily strategy.

Directions for Activity Grid Use:

There are 10 blank lines down the left side of the activity grid. This is where you will write the specific daily tasks that support your destination and support you in being the best you that you can be. Here is a sample of what it might look like:

- Time with God
- Time with family
- Exercise
- Eat healthfully
- 10 attempts to schedule new prospects
- 10 attempts to follow up
- Return e-mails
- 20 minutes to declutter and organize
- Journal
- 20 minutes of professional education (reading)

Be sure to keep each activity in the realm of your control. By this I mean activities that you actually control, like dialing the phone. Some will try to put outcomes on the activity grid, and that is a road to frustration. For example, you might put "$200 in sales" or "3 selling appointments" on one of the lines. This simply is not going to work because it is an attempt to control outcome. You don't have control here. There is no control over who will answer your calls, what the person will say if he or she answers the phone, and that the person will say "yes" to you in a way that you would like him or her to.

It is important to list the activities that support your destination, but it is also important to make sure you are listing some things that take care of you so that you can be the best person that you can be. These are things like exercise, eating healthfully, time with God, etc. Use whatever works for you.

You may not have 10 things that you can identify to fill in all the lines. That is okay. Don't get hung up on that. You may identify things later that need to be placed on the list. Add as you go.

As you complete each task every day, check it off on the corresponding circle to the right of the task listed. The activity grid will last one week. If you begin to notice that there are one or two tasks not getting done consistently, it is time to take a look at that.

What is the big stop? What needs to change for you to get these tasks done? Are you procrastinating? Use the formula to neutralize procrastination. Are you piling too much on, that is, being unrealistic about what you can do in the given time? Some people have a habit of having higher expectations about their allotted time than others.

The bottom of the activity grid has some squares with the words "Big Win" in them. You want to write a synchronicity, blessing, or miracle in these boxes each day. They happen all around us every day, and we simply have to be in tune to them. Maybe you met some outstanding people or just had an overall happy day. Write it down, because no synchronicity or blessing is too small to mention.

Balance and flow is key in all things.

Day 3

Look at your activity grid. What have you done so far today? Check off all that you have done. Think about when you are going to do the remainder. Are you noticing any changes in your thinking or activity so far?

What landmark will tell you that you are on track for your destination at Day 30? Day 60? Go to those days in the journal and write down your landmark.

Day 3 (continued)

Make sure you are giving yourself time to rest and re-create.

Day 4

Before departing on any journey, the proper tools and accessories must be packed. Let's begin with a winning attitude and daily thought process.

I AM...

Develop affirmations to support you in moving toward your destination.

These need to be stated in the present tense.

Examples:
"I am looking fine in my new suit!"
"I am feeling better and better each day"
"I am reaching my destination with ease, grace, and joy!"

Check out some of my favorite "I am" statements in the reference section at the back of this book.

Take time each day to sit with these. Move into that moment of "I am"—move into God Space. Choose one or two statements to focus on each day.

God is the great "I am"!

"I AM..."

Journal your affirmations here.
Pick one or two per day to carry in your thoughts.

Do your "I am" statements feel doable?
Do they feel believable?
Does that undertow in the back of your head chime in when you say some of your affirmations?
If so, restate them here as "allow" statements.

Example:

"I allow myself the experience of purchasing and wearing my new suit."

"I allow abundance to flow into my life with ease, grace, and joy."

I ALLOW...

_____

_____

_____

_____

_____

_____

_____

_____

_____

_____

Day 5

When you reach your destination, how will you reward yourself or celebrate? Take a moment to plan your celebration. Now, write it in your day planner on your Day 90 page.

I am/allow

_____

I am/allow

_____

Day 6

Continue with the "I am" statements.

I am/allow

_____

I am/allow

_____

Take the time to be a student of your life.

What are you learning about yourself as you settle into a new way of being? Do you find yourself beginning to let yourself off of the hook for anything on the activity grid or putting off any of the activities?

_____

_____

_____

_____

_____

Day 7

What is your operating "frequency" most of the time? Where are you mentally living/thinking most of the time? Is there something you need to release so that you can live more lightly?

Where are the people around you living mentally much of the time? Are you subscribing to their mental lives? Are you isolating yourself? Why or why not?

I am/allow

_____

I am/allow

_____

Use the following page to identify any undertow. Write down all negative thoughts and feelings that go through your mind on any given day. You may add to the sheet as you think of them. False beliefs qualify for this as well. Let the next page represent the box that your undertow tries to keep you in.

It might hold statements like this:

> "My thighs are fat."
> "You will never amount to anything."
> "I am too hot-headed."
> "I am a poor money manager."
> "Reaching the next level in my career is hard."

You get the idea. Remember, we are just exposing the box so that we can recognize false thoughts when we think them. It helps to know when the negative mind chatter flows in so that we can look at it and disregard it as we choose to move on down the path toward the destination. Empty your vessel of the negative mind chatter so that you can begin the process of refilling it with good stuff.

The Zen of attraction: "Less is more."
—Thomas Leonard, founder, Coach U and Coachville.com

My box of undertow

Day 8

Step out of your self-imposed box! Remember:

1. Get clear about your intention

2. Think optimally

3. Focus on what you want

4. Believe and have faith

5. Persevere

6. Celebrate

7. Be grateful

As you read the above list, make some notes beside each one about what it looks like to you. Think of it this way: based on a scale from 0 to 10, with 0 meaning that it is nonexistent and 10 meaning that it is there all of the time, what would the difference look and feel like in your life?

I am/allow

_____

I am/allow

_____

> "Don't believe everything you think!"
> —THE CARTOON CHARACTER, MAXINE

Day 9

Where did you mentally live for most of the day today? Were you focused in the present moment, or did you focus on past events and potential future consequences? Journal some thoughts here.

_____

_____

_____

_____

_____

_____

_____

_____

_____

_____

I am/allow

_____

I am/allow

_____

Day 10

How is the activity grid going? Are there activities that are consistently being overlooked? What is getting in the way or distracting you? What is capturing your attention/focus? Where you focus is expanding. What step do you need to take right now to gain movement toward your destination?

Create some energy. Take out the Energy Leaks List. Begin jotting down the drains and distractions in your life. This is the first step in eliminating them. Each day, take a step in the direction of eliminating one. For example, if clutter is a problem, set a timer for 20 minutes per day to focus on decluttering an area. If it is another person, what boundaries do you need to establish? Check the reference section for readings on subjects like boundaries and organization.

I am/allow

_____

I am/allow

_____

Did you set the tone for your day?
Start with nourishing mind, body, and spirit!
Be a student of your life.

Day 11

Happiness and Joy are an inside job. Begin setting the stage for each day. When you wake up every day, take a few minutes to picture yourself at your destination. Feel it. Smell it. Hear it. See it. Be it.

Set your joy scale to 10. Supercharge the path to your destination! The joy scale is rated on a range of 0 to 10.

0 = Yuck

10 = Happy, Happy, Happy! Heaven on Earth!

Your body and energy follow where you focus. Journal what you notice about this exercise. What do you see, feel, smell, hear, etc.? Does your undertow attempt to pull you away from what you want? Notice if you found it difficult to get to 10 on the joy scale. If so, relax. Not everyone masters this right away. Keep practicing. It is like going to the gym; you have to be consistent to build the muscle.

I am/allow

_____

I am/allow

_____

Joy Scale = _____

You are the driver of your mind—it does not drive you.

Day 12

By now, you may be noticing some roadblocks or distractions on your path. Is it procrastination? Do you need to practice the Three Rs? Revisit the tools provided in the first half of the book.

What is stopping *You*?

_____

_____

What needs to shift/change to go around or over any roadblocks?

_____

_____

What do you choose?

_____

_____

If you are experiencing flow and synchronicities, Congratulations! Write about them here.

_____

_____

_____

_____

Day 12 (continued)

_____

_____

_____

_____

_____

_____

_____

_____

_____

_____

Continue to choose two affirmations each day.

I am/allow

_____

I am/allow

_____

Joy Scale = _____

Day 13

Are you putting off change? Schedule a change for yourself. Schedule a win! Take just one step in the direction of success. Maybe you choose to make more calls or give yourself some down time. Whatever it is, plan it and do it!

If you are in flow, how is this feeling?

_____

_____

What are you noticing about your internal environment? Your feelings?

_____

_____

Schedule your power partner to do the "as if" exercise. This will supercharge the path to your destination! The "as if" instructions are in the *Accelerate on the Path to Success* section of the book.

I am/allow

_____

I am/allow

_____

Where was your joy scale after your "as if" exercise?

_____

Make a commitment to yourself!

Day 14

139

If your undertow is too loud, visualize it as a cartoon or movie character. Picture yourself locking it in a trunk or a closet, or leaving it on the side of the road somewhere. Put it away to continue down your path to success!

I am/allow

_____

I am/allow

_____

Joy Scale = _____

"Get out of your self-imposed box!"

Day 15

How is the activity grid consistency going? Are you checking off your activities consistently? If not, what is the payoff for avoiding some of the activities? What keeps you from changing this pattern of behavior? What emotions surface at the thought of change?

Remember, you may not check off everything on your activity grid every day. You simply want to make sure that you are not avoiding any single activity for more than two days.

I am/allow

_____

I am/allow

_____

Joy Scale = _____

Day 16

Here is the formula to neutralize procrastination. Use it!

1. Stop and think!

2. "I don't want to do this (whatever you are avoiding) because

   _____."

3. What am I telling myself to continue procrastinating?

4. What evidence do I have proving any of that to be true? (the above mind chatter)

5. What am I risking by staying frozen in procrastination?

6. What am I risking by taking a step forward toward my success?

7. What am I willing to do right now?

Copy this and carry with you. It gets easier as you use it, because you go right into action and quit analyzing the moment of decision.

I am/allow

_____

I am/allow

_____

Joy Scale = _____

Day 17

I am/allow

_____

I am/allow

_____

Joy Scale = _____

Have any time and energy vampires been eliminated at this point? Do any need to be added to the list for future elimination?

_____

_____

_____

_____

Day 18

What are you willing to do right now? Staying in procrastination, or the box, is safe, familiar, and predictable. On the menu of your life, what do you choose today—safety or success?

I am/allow

_____

I am/allow

_____

Joy Scale = _____

Are You...

1. Clear about the intention?

2. Thinking optimally?

3. Focused on what you want?

4. Believing and having faith?

5. Persevering?

6. Celebrating?

7. Being grateful?

Day 19

Who are you "being" today? If you want more of something in life, be that person today. For example, if you want more money, be the blessing of abundance to someone.

If you want more balance, take the time to "be" balanced today.

If you want more time, give yourself or someone else the gift of 15 minutes today.

Notice how what you want shows up when you make space in your life for it to enter. If you never make space for the things you want, they cannot get into your life.

I am/allow

_____

I am/allow

_____

Joy Scale = _____

The good things will enter your life only when there is room.

Day 20

Whhat did you choose today—safety or success?

Journal events here.

_____

_____

_____

_____

_____

_____

What synchronicities showed up for you today?

_____

_____

_____

_____

I am/allow

_____

I am/allow

_____

Joy Scale = _____

If more cash flow is what you want in your life, write a letter to Money. If Money were a friend of yours, what would you say to it?

Dear Money,
 I miss you! Bring all of your big friends and move in with me! I am sorry that I have been kicking you out of my bank account so much, please forgive me.
  Sincerely,
  Me

Dear Money,

_____

_____

_____

_____

_____

_____

Day 21

Pay attention to who and what you are "being" today. That inner environment is of utmost importance in this transformation.

What synchronicities seem to be showing up for you?
Are you noticing patterns in your life that may or may not serve you?

Common patterns for some:
- People who say one thing and do another (lack of integrity)
- Illness
- Series of traffic violations or accidents
- Missed details
- People and events showing up in perfect timing to take you to the next step
- Money appearing out of seemingly nowhere (money found in laundry, on the ground, in coat pockets, etc.)

Look for the hidden value in your life. Did the letter to money show you how you are treating it? Your attitude toward it?

I am/allow

_____

I am/allow

_____

Joy Scale = _____

Did you visualize your destination today?

Day 22

Take note of any undertow that shows up often to pull you away from what you want. What emotion seems to accompany the undertow most often? Fear, guilt, sadness, anger, etc.?

Mastering emotions is important, because emotions can rule the thinking processes, which in turn prompt behavior. Think about how emotions can prompt impulsiveness, which can lead to getting off the path to success. Impulsiveness and emotions can show up in spending habits, eating habits, relationship decisions, health habits, as well as a myriad of other areas. Is there an area that you wish to master?

Practice the three Rs.

Check out the box you completed on Day 7: is there anything you are able to cross off because it no longer rules you?

_____

_____

I am/allow

_____

I am/allow

_____

Today's synchronicities:

_____

_____

Visualized my destination!
Supercharged my destination—Joy Scale = _____

Day 23

Learn more about an area that you wish to master. No matter what the subject, obtain information. Listen to books on CD, read magazines, books, and websites. Challenge the beliefs being held around the subject. For example:

Are you thinking that investments are only for those who already have a lot of money? Do you believe you cannot accumulate wealth because you are in a dead-end job? Do you think that you will always be overweight because your parents are? Have you convinced yourself that you are the victim of bad genes? Are you focused into struggling in life?

Explore what beliefs are holding you back. Remember, you create your outward reality with the beliefs you hold in your inner reality.

Your box may be screaming at you if you are starting to deconstruct false personal beliefs. What did you learn today?

_____

_____

I am/allow

_____

I am/allow

_____

Today's synchronicities:

_____

_____

Visualized my destination!
Supercharged my destination—Joy Scale = _____

Day 24

Be in God Space today. What does your mind do when you sit down to be quiet? Does it get noisy and begin to drift off to the day's events? Come back to center and focus on the "I am" statements you have chosen for the day.

Write your thoughts about this. Use some feeling words here. Remember, your feelings supercharge your thoughts.

_____

_____

_____

_____

_____

I am/allow

_____

I am/allow

_____

Today's synchronicities:

_____

_____

Visualized my destination!
Supercharged my destination—Joy Scale = _____

Day 25

I am/allow

_____

I am/allow

_____

Today's synchronicities:

_____

_____

Visualized my destination!
Supercharged my destination—Joy Scale = _____

Day 26

I am/allow

_____

I am/allow

_____

Today's synchronicities:

_____

_____

Visualized my destination!
Supercharged my destination—Joy Scale = _____

What did you learn about you or any subject today?

_____

_____

_____

_____

_____

Nourish mind, body, and spirit!

Day 27

Are you developing a new definition of you? If so, what is changing? Are you aware of the changes in your internal environment? Your confidence is like a tropical plant. It needs nurturing and warmth. If your internal environment is cold and sterile, how can your confidence grow? Be kind to you: nurture yourself. Negative self-talk is not conducive to a warm climate.

Perfectionism is an attitude of lack and creates a cold inner environment. Perfectionists are constantly focused on what is wrong or what isn't good enough, so their focus expands in lack. Remember, what you focus on is expanding. Where you focus is where you are investing. What compels you to invest in what you don't want?

_____

_____

_____

I am/allow

_____

I am/allow

_____

Today's synchronicities:

_____

_____

Visualized my destination!
Supercharged my destination—Joy Scale = _____

Day 28

I am/allow

_____

I am/allow

_____

Today's synchronicities:

_____

_____

Did the "as if" exercise with my power partner.
Supercharged my destination—Joy Scale = _____

Day 29

I am/allow

_____

I am/allow

_____

Today's synchronicities:

_____

_____

Visualized my destination!
Supercharged my destination—Joy Scale = _____

Are You:

1. Clear about the intention?

2. Thinking optimally?

3. Focused on what you want?

4. Believing and having faith?

5. Persevering?

6. Celebrating?

7. Being grateful?

Day 30

Landmark: What old beliefs about you are starting to fade away?

_____

_____

What new beliefs about you do you want to embrace further today?

_____

_____

What one step (and probably large step) are you willing to take today to move toward your destination?

_____

I am/allow

_____

I am/allow

_____

Today's synchronicities:

_____

_____

Made my blessings charge card! (Cut out a credit card–sized piece of card stock. Write 10 blessings in your life and read it to charge yourself up!)
Supercharged my destination—Joy Scale = _____

Day 31

Where are you in relation to the landmark you set for Day 30? Are you there? Is it in sight, or are you struggling to see it? Why or why not?

_____

_____

_____

_____

I am/allow

_____

I am/allow

_____

Today's synchronicities:

_____

_____

Visualized my destination!
Supercharged my destination—Joy Scale = _____

The only thing you have control over is moment-to-moment activity. Focus on that and keep on moving forward.

"The pursuit of dreams can be more fun than the acquisition"
—Dave Huber

Day 32

Today is an opportunity to "be" different and get different results. Based on where you found yourself in relation to your landmark, this may or may not pertain to you. If you are feeling behind in reaching the 30-day landmark, it's okay. Don't get caught up in the old paradigm that more work equals more productivity or better results. Beating yourself up about it won't help either. How can you work smarter toward your destination? What opportunities are you not taking advantage of?

_____

_____

_____

_____

I am/allow

_____

I am/allow

_____

Today's synchronicities:

_____

_____

Visualized my destination!
Supercharged my destination—Joy Scale = _____

Day 33

I am/allow

_____

I am/allow

_____

Today's synchronicities:

_____

_____

Visualized my destination!
Supercharged my destination—Joy Scale = _____

What did you learn today? Be a student of your life.

Day 34

I am/allow

_____

I am/allow

_____

Today's synchronicities:

_____

_____

Visualized my destination!
Supercharged my destination—Joy Scale = _____

Day 35

Are you practicing the three Rs when the undertow creeps in?

    Recognize it…

    Release it…

    Replace it…

I am/allow

_____

I am/allow

_____

Today's synchronicities:

_____

_____

Visualized my destination!
Supercharged my destination—Joy Scale = _____
Stayed with the power partner and "as if" exercise!

    The more you live there mentally, the closer the destination gets!

Day 36

Are you listening to your head or your heart? What is the difference, you may ask? Think about a time when you felt compelled to do or say something and you didn't know why. You did it, and it was the right thing to say or do at the right time. That is your heart speaking—an indication that you are listening to God.

Our heads can jump in and get us stuck in analysis paralysis. We justify, procrastinate, and begin asking everyone around us what we *should* do. Should carries guilt. I am not suggesting that you go out and bet your life savings, but I am suggesting that you listen to what feels right in your heart or spirit, because God is talking to us on a regular basis. You just have to decide to be quiet and listen! We can't listen if we are busy talking, either audibly or mentally.

Write about a time that you chose to listen to your heart. What happened? How did you feel? Were you at peace? Did your head try to jump in and talk you in or out of anything at the time? What is your heart telling you right now? What is it that you see is your next step according to your heart? Sometimes, the right thing to do is the hardest thing to do.

I am/allow

_____

I am/allow

_____

Today's synchronicities:

_____

_____

Visualized my destination!
Supercharged my destination—Joy Scale = _____

Day 37

I am/allow

_____

I am/allow

_____

Today's synchronicities:

_____

_____

Visualized my destination!
Supercharged my destination—Joy Scale = _____

Day 38

I am/allow

_____

I am/allow

_____

Today's synchronicities:

_____

_____

Updated my blessings charge card!
Supercharged my destination—Joy Scale = _____

Day 39

I am/allow

_____

I am/allow

_____

Today's synchronicities:

_____

_____

Visualized my destination!
Supercharged my destination—Joy Scale = _____

    Are there any energy leaks to work on eliminating? Get rid of them and gain energy.

    Are you looking at your activity grid daily? Stay focused on the destination!

Day 40

I am/allow

_____

I am/allow

_____

Today's synchronicities:

_____

_____

Visualized my destination!
Supercharged my destination—Joy Scale = _____

Day 41

I am/allow

_____

I am/allow

_____

Today's synchronicities:

_____

_____

Visualized my destination!
Supercharged my destination—Joy Scale = _____

Read Matthew 21:22 and think about where
your mind is much of the time.

Day 42

I am/allow

_____

I am/allow

_____

Today's synchronicities:

_____

_____

Visualized my destination!

    Today, put a new twist on the visualization. If you want more money in your life, try this visualization. It is a lot of fun! Close your eyes and get relaxed. Imagine that the windows in your home all fly open at the same time and 100-dollar bills are flying into your home through every window. They are piling up in your home, and you are literally rolling in them. You can smell them, feel them, and see them. Note your feelings right now.

Supercharged my destination—Joy Scale = _____

Day 43

I am/allow

_____

I am/allow

_____

Today's synchronicities:

_____

_____

Visualized my destination!
Supercharged my destination—Joy Scale = _____

Set the tone for your day!
Nourish mind, body, and spirit!

Day 44

What has captured your focus and attention most today? Do you find yourself in perpetual motion and "busyness," looking very busy, but not accomplishing much of anything?

I am/allow

_____

I am/allow

_____

Today's synchronicities:

_____

_____

Visualized my destination!
Supercharged my destination—Joy Scale = _____

Day 45

I am/allow

_____

I am/allow

_____

Today's synchronicities:

_____

_____

Visualized my destination!
Supercharged my destination—Joy Scale = _____

Day 46

You are halfway to your destination! What have you learned about yourself in the journey toward your destination so far? Are some days better than others? What support structures need to be put in place for the days that feel challenging?

_____

_____

_____

How is the activity grid working for you?

Have you uncovered any new false thoughts or beliefs to add to your box of undertow? Are you able to cross anything off in your box?

Are you living in God Space with the synchronicities? Are you walking toward the destination with blind faith, or are you doubting along the way? Doubt weakens faith and the energy we invest in the destination.

Day 47

How is the energy leak list coming along? Have you looked at it or added to it lately? If not, take a look and see if there are any steps you can take to continue the process of elimination. Eliminating these gives you energy, which you can use for other endeavors. Go for it!

I am/allow

_____

I am/allow

_____

Today's synchronicities:

_____

_____

Visualized my destination!
Supercharged my destination—Joy Scale = _____

Day 48

I am/allow

_____

I am/allow

_____

Today's synchronicities:

_____

_____

Visualized my destination!
Supercharged my destination—Joy Scale = _____

Make room for the good things in life

Day 49

I am/allow

_____

I am/allow

_____

Today's synchronicities:

_____

_____

Visualized my destination!
Supercharged my destination—Joy Scale = _____

Be sure to:

1. Get clear about the intention

2. Think optimally

3. Focus on what you want

4. Believe and have faith

5. Persevere

6. Celebrate

7. Be grateful

Day 50

I am/allow

_____

I am/allow

_____

Today's synchronicities:

_____

_____

Visualized my destination!
Supercharged my destination—Joy Scale = _____

Day 51

I am/allow

_____

I am/allow

_____

Today's synchronicities:

_____

_____

Stayed with the "as if" exercise and my power partner!
Supercharged my destination—Joy Scale = _____

Day 52

I am/allow

_____

I am/allow

_____

Today's synchronicities:

_____

_____

Visualized my destination!
Supercharged my destination—Joy Scale = _____

Day 53

I am/allow

_____

I am/allow

_____

Today's synchronicities:

_____

_____

Visualized my destination!
Supercharged my destination—Joy Scale = _____

How can you nourish mind and spirit today?
Take just a few minutes to do this.

Day 54

Release your fear; it is probably nothing more than your box talking. Who do you want to give your power to—greatness and glory, or fear and scarcity? You choose.

I am/allow

_____

I am/allow

_____

Today's synchronicities:

_____

_____

Visualized my destination!
Supercharged my destination—Joy Scale = _____

Day 55

Are you feeling the momentum? Why or why not? Take a quantum leap today. Tuck your fear under your arm and run!

I am/allow

_____

I am/allow

_____

Today's synchronicities:

_____

_____

Visualized my destination!
Supercharged my destination—Joy Scale = _____

Start the day with nourishment for mind, body, and spirit.

Day 56

I am/allow

_____

I am/allow

_____

Today's synchronicities:

_____

_____

Visualized my destination!
Supercharged my destination—Joy Scale = _____

Day 57

I am/allow

___

I am/allow

___

Today's synchronicities:

___

___

Visualized my destination!
Supercharged my destination—Joy Scale = _____

Day 58

I am/allow

_____

I am/allow

_____

Today's synchronicities:

_____

_____

Visualized my destination! Get into the moment of winning! Supercharged my destination—Joy Scale = _____

Day 59

What is that you want and just can't see with your eyes yet?

I am/allow

_____

I am/allow

_____

Today's synchronicities:

_____

_____

Visualized my destination!
Supercharged my destination—Joy Scale = _____

Day 60

You are two-thirds of the way to your destination! Congratulations! Do you feel on track with the landmark you set in the beginning? Why or why not? If you are still feeling behind, let's take a long, hard look at this. What is the struggle about? What needs to change for this situation to move into alignment with you? Remember, the only person you can change is you. What feels challenging to you right now? What needs to change so that there is flow right now? What are you winning at, big-time, right now? What would give you a quantum leap forward and bring peace right now?

I am/allow

_____

I am/allow

_____

Today's synchronicities:

_____

_____

Visualized my destination!
Supercharged my destination—Joy Scale = _____

Day 61

What do you need to shift or let go of to make room for what you want? Often, it is your false personal beliefs that need to shift or be released, because they are what hold your dreams and destinations at bay.

I am/allow

_____

I am/allow

_____

Today's synchronicities:

_____

_____

Visualized my destination!
Supercharged my destination—Joy Scale = _____

Day 62

I am/allow

_____

I am/allow

_____

Today's synchronicities:

_____

_____

Charge yourself up with your blessings charge card!
Supercharged my destination—Joy Scale = _____

Day 63

What new awareness do you have?

I am/allow

_____

I am/allow

_____

Today's synchronicities:

_____

_____

Visualized my destination!
Supercharged my destination—Joy Scale = _____

Day 64

I am/allow

_____

I am/allow

_____

Today's synchronicities:

_____

_____

Visualized my destination!
Supercharged my destination—Joy Scale = _____

Start with a balanced and nourishing tone today.

Day 65

I am/allow

_____

I am/allow

_____

Today's synchronicities:

_____

_____

Visualized my destination!
Supercharged my destination—Joy Scale = _____

Day 66

I am/allow

_____

I am/allow

_____

Today's synchronicities:

_____

_____

Visualized my destination!
Supercharged my destination—Joy Scale = _____

Day 67

I am/allow

_____

I am/allow

_____

Today's synchronicities:

_____

_____

Visualized my destination!
Supercharged my destination—Joy Scale = _____

Day 68

I am/allow

_____

I am/allow

_____

Today's synchronicities:

_____

_____

Visualized my destination!
Supercharged my destination—Joy Scale = _____

1. Get clear about the intention

2. Think optimally

3. Focus on what you want

4. Believe and have faith

5. Persevere

6. Celebrate

7. Be grateful

Day 69

I am/allow

_____

I am/allow

_____

Today's synchronicities:

_____

_____

Did an "as if" exercise with my power partner today!
Supercharged my destination—Joy Scale = _____

Be _____
Do _____
Have _____

Day 70

I am/allow

_____

I am/allow

_____

Today's synchronicities:

_____

_____

Visualized my destination!
Supercharged my destination—Joy Scale = _____

Day 71

I am/allow

_____

I am/allow

_____

Today's synchronicities:

_____

_____

Visualized my destination!
Supercharged my destination—Joy Scale = _____

You are what you believe!

Day 72

If you are feeling behind on your journey, it's okay. Just continue down the path. Stopping is not going to get you any closer. Don't move into all-or-nothing thinking. All-or-nothing thinking looks like this: "If I can't do it right or 100 percent, I won't do anything at all!"

Take steps in spite of what your undertow is telling you. If you have had the all-or-nothing thoughts, add them to your box. These thoughts are another angle that it can no longer use.

I am/allow

_____

I am/allow

_____

Today's synchronicities:

_____

_____

Visualized my destination!
Supercharged my destination—Joy Scale = _____

Day 73

I am/allow

_____

I am/allow

_____

Today's synchronicities:

_____

_____

Visualized my destination! Saw it. Felt it. Smelled it. Heard it. Supercharged my destination—Joy Scale = _____

Day 74

I am/allow

_____

I am/allow

_____

Today's synchronicities:

_____

_____

Visualized my destination!
Supercharged my destination—Joy Scale = _____

Day 75

Stay in your integrity. You told yourself that you wanted this destination, so keep moving toward it! Even if you feel behind, you are on course toward it and keeping your word. If you are ahead of schedule, celebrate!

I am/allow

_____

I am/allow

_____

Today's synchronicities:

_____

_____

Called my "as if" partner!
Visualized my destination!
Supercharged my destination—Joy Scale = _____

Day 76

I am/allow

_____

I am/allow

_____

Today's synchronicities:

_____

_____

Visualized my destination!
Supercharged my destination—Joy Scale = _____

1. Get clear about the intention

2. Think optimally

3. Focus on what you want

4. Believe and have faith

5. Persevere

6. Celebrate

7. Be grateful

Day 77

I am/allow

_____

I am/allow

_____

Today's synchronicities:

_____

_____

Visualized my destination!
Supercharged my destination—Joy Scale = _____

Day 78

I am/allow

_____

I am/allow

_____

Today's synchronicities:

_____

_____

Visualized my destination!
Supercharged my destination—Joy Scale = _____

Day 79

I am/allow

_____

I am/allow

_____

Today's synchronicities:

_____

_____

Visualized my destination!
Supercharged my destination—Joy Scale = _____

Day 80

Only 10 days to go!! Feeling the momentum? Focus on the daily activity and pick up the pace.

I am/allow

_____

I am/allow

_____

Today's synchronicities:

_____

_____

Visualized my destination!
Supercharged my destination—Joy Scale = _____

Day 81

I am/allow

_____

I am/allow

_____

Today's synchronicities:

_____

_____

Visualized my destination!
Supercharged my destination—Joy Scale = _____

Be _____
Do _____
Have _____

Day 82

I am/allow

_____

I am/allow

_____

Today's synchronicities:

_____

_____

Visualized my destination!
Supercharged my destination—Joy Scale = _____

1. Get clear about the intention

2. Think optimally

3. Focus on what you want

4. Believe and have faith

5. Persevere

6. Celebrate

7. Be grateful

Day 83

What do you need to stretch for this week? Write it down and use this in your daily "I am/allow" statements.

I am/allow

_____

I am/allow

_____

Today's synchronicities:

_____

_____

Visualized my destination!
Supercharged my destination—Joy Scale = _____

Day 84

Who are you "being"?

I am/allow

_____

I am/allow

_____

Today's synchronicities:

_____

_____

Visualized my destination!
Supercharged my destination—Joy Scale = _____

Day 85

I am/allow

_____

I am/allow

_____

Today's synchronicities:

_____

_____

Visualized my destination!
Supercharged my destination—Joy Scale = _____

Day 86

Are you stretching for the finish line? Keep up the good work!

I am/allow

_____

I am/allow

_____

Today's synchronicities:

_____

_____

Did the "as if" exercise with my power partner today! Supercharged my destination—Joy Scale = _____

Be _____
Do _____
Have _____

Day 87

I am/allow

_____

I am/allow

_____

Today's synchronicities:

_____

_____

Visualized my destination!
Supercharged my destination—Joy Scale = _____

Day 88

I am/allow

_____

I am/allow

_____

Today's synchronicities:

_____

_____

Visualized my destination!
Supercharged my destination—Joy Scale = _____

Day 89

You're almost there! Prepare to celebrate! What final touches need to be put in place to finish with ease, grace, and joy? What are you willing to stretch for today?

I am/allow

_____

I am/allow

_____

Today's synchronicities:

_____

_____

Visualized my destination!
Supercharged my destination—Joy Scale = _____

Day 90

You did it! Congratulations! Celebrate!

What did you learn on this journey?

_____

_____

_____

_____

What did you learn about *you* on this journey?

_____

_____

_____

_____

What beliefs did you find were false? What did you replace them with?

_____

_____

_____

_____

Call your "as if" partner and celebrate!
E-mail *coachlora@hotmail.com* to announce your arrival!

Part 4

Resources

RESOURCES

I have listed some great reading resources. If you choose to take advice from these sources, it is just that—your choice. The idea in listing these is for you to continue being a student of your life and to get out of your self-imposed box!

The ADHD Fraud: How Psychiatry Makes "Patients" Out Of Normal Children by Fred A. Baughman Jr., M.D., *www.adhdfraud.org*

The Antidepressant Solution by Joseph Glenmullen, M.D., Free Press, New York, 2005.

The Biology of Belief by Bruce Lipton, Ph.D., Elite Books, Santa Rosa, California, 2005.

Boundaries by Dr. Henry Cloud and Dr. John Townsend, Zondervan, Grand Rapids, Michigan, 2002.

Choice Theory: A New Psychology Of Personal Freedom by William Glasser, M.D., Harper Collins, New York, 1998.

Claim Your Victory Today by Dr. Creflo A. Dollar, Warner Faith Hachette Book Group USA, New York, 2006.

Daily Readings from Your Best Life Now: 90 Devotions for Living at Your Fullest Potential. Joel Osteen Publishing, 2005.

Dreaming Your Way To Pain-Free Living: From Chronic Pain To Complete Relief In Six Months by Neil McHugh 2006, *www.painfreeliving.org*

EFT—Emotional Freedom Techniques. Emotional Freedom Techniques are painless, quick, and usually have lasting results. There are no drugs and no needles in this process. Release old, painful patterns in as little as one session as well as eliminate negative emotional "knots" that sabotage your best efforts in achieving success. Kim McHugh, EFT-CC, EFT-ADV, EFTpractitioner@yahoo.com

Everything You Need to Know to Feel Go(o)d by Candace B. Pert, Ph.D., Hay House, California, 2006.

Excuse Me, Your Life Is Waiting by Lynn Grabhorn, Hampton Roads Publishing Company, Inc., 2000.

File It Pro! www.fileit-pro.com Software to help with your office filing and operations needs.

The Five Love Languages: How to Express Heartfelt Commitment to Your Mate by Gary Chapman, Northfield Publishing, 1995.

www.flylady.net All the information necessary to get organized.

Hormones, Health, and Happiness by Steven F. Hotze, M.D., Forrest, Austin, Texas, 2005.

Jesus, CEO by Laurie Beth Jones, Hyperion, New York, 1995.

Life in the Word by Joyce Meyer, Harrison House, Inc., Tulsa, Oklahoma, 1998.

Lita Lee, Ph.D. *www.litalee.com* Learn what enzymes can do for you.

Molecules Of Emotion by Candace B. Pert, Ph.D., Scribners, New York, 1997.

New Pathways Health & Wellness Center, Springfield, Missouri

www.newpathwayshwc.com (417) 844-6283

Ray Peat, Ph.D., *www.raypeat.com* Interesting reading about hormones and other issues related to health.

The Science of Getting Rich by Wallace D. Wattles, *www.scienceofgettingrich.net*

Secrets of The Millionaire Mind by T. Harv Eker, Harper Business, New York, 2005.

The Total Money Makeover: A Proven Plan for Financial Fitness by Dave Ramsey, Thomas Nelson Publishers, 2003.

Think Before You Look: Avoiding the Consequences of Secret Temptation by Daniel Henderson,

Living Ink Books, Chattanooga, Tennessee, 2005.

Warning: Psychiatry Can Be Hazardous To Your Mental Health by William Glasser, M.D.,

Harper Collins, New York, 2003.

Your Body Is Your Subconscious Mind by Candace B. Pert, Ph.D. (audio book)

Biblical references taken from *Holy Bible: New International Version.* Copyright 1973, 1978, 1984 by International Bible Society. All rights reserved worldwide.

Part 5

Appendix

APPENDIX

T/K

Appendix

YOUR ENERGY LEAKS

We all have something that is draining us. It might be the squeaky wheel of the car, dusty shelves, cluttered closets, and yes, even the behavior of other people. What are you putting up with? What is draining you of valuable energy, time, and space? List these "drains and distractions" on this page and take steps each day toward eliminating them!

1. _____
2. _____
3. _____
4. _____
5. _____
6. _____
7. _____
8. _____
9. _____
10. _____

11. _____

12. _____

13. _____

14. _____

15. _____

16. _____

17. _____

18. _____

19. _____

20. _____

©Copyright 2004 Life University Coaching

Some of My Favorite "I Am" Statements:

I now choose to release limiting beliefs about money and abundance. I am living abundantly, and money flows freely to me with ease, grace, and joy!

I am healthy and strong.

I am perfect just as I am, because I am a creation of God.

I choose to move through this with ease, grace, and joy. (I use this when I feel frustrated and/or confused.)

I am embracing and enjoying the overflow of blessings in my life!

I am thankful for _____.

Remember to always supercharge an "I am" statement by visualizing yourself in it and experiencing how that feels. Make it real!

Activity	Monday	Tuesday	Wednesday	Thursday	Friday	Saturday	Sunday
1	☺	☺	☺	☺	☺	☺	☺
2	☺	☺	☺	☺	☺	☺	☺
3	☺	☺	☺	☺	☺	☺	☺
4	☺	☺	☺	☺	☺	☺	☺
5	☺	☺	☺	☺	☺	☺	☺
6	☺	☺	☺	☺	☺	☺	☺
7	☺	☺	☺	☺	☺	☺	☺
8	☺	☺	☺	☺	☺	☺	☺
9	☺	☺	☺	☺	☺	☺	☺
10	☺	☺	☺	☺	☺	☺	☺

Monday	Tuesday	Wednesday	Thursday	Friday	Saturday	Sunday
☺	☺	☺	☺	☺	☺	☺

Big Win!